Soul Searchers MEDITATION

ANY TIME - ANY WHERE

Second Edition

R. Venugopalan

HEALTH HARMONY

An imprint of

B. Jain Publishers (P) Ltd.

An ISO 9001 : 2000 Certified Company

Soul searchers

Meditation any time any where

Second Edition: 2006

Reprint Edition: Oct. 2006

Published by Kuldeep Jain for

HEALTH HARMONY

1921, Street No. 10, Chuna Mandi, Paharganj,
New Delhi 110 055 (INDIA)
Ph. : 91-11-23583100, 23581300, 23581100, 23580800, 51698991
Fax : 91-11-23580471, 51698993
Email : bjain@vsnl.com
Website : www.bjainbooks.com

Printed in India by

J.J. OFFSET PRINTERS
522, FIE, Patpar Ganj, Delhi-110092

ISBN : 81-8056-371-5
BOOKCODE: BV-5724

Preface

He who wanders the streets of his own inner self is able to derive the most from the eternal light and is provided a chance to merge with the cosmic being.

Mysterious is the universe, and still more magical is the working of the universal Lord. Imagine the continuance working of two sides of one coin, one representing the tamasic people, whose only interest in the materialistic benefits and the other side representing the Rajasic people, whose interest have been spilt into two one related to the spiritual aspect and the other material aspect. They continuously work on the sides of the nature and the central aspect represents the Sattvic nature. This nature is the exact opposite of Tamasic nature; here individuals have full faith in the spiritual aspect of life.

Most of the time people never try hard to understand the purpose of their existence and the goal of life. It is only those who try hard understand that Self-Realisation is the most beautiful experience that a person can have in this world of illusion. This realisation is an omnipotent essence of the Universal Lord. Man of worldly nature spends precious time in finding happiness in the illusory world of material benefits and gains. He tries to pacify his desires by worldly things like wealth, fame, title etc., but in the end finds himself worn out with neither peace, harmony within himself. He even starts reaching the epoch centre of learning for finding peace but here again he finds cult worshippers, spiritualism packaged and sold in a colourful commercial manner.

For gaining peace of mind he wanders through the streets of darkness by consuming liquor, drugs and other intoxicating materials, and then in the later stages tries to run away from himself.

But none provides him the solace and peace, because it cannot be found outside it is from within that you get peace. Look within and then only you realise that the whole world is nothing more than a playground where everyone has lost track of the original path, those who finds it release himself from the agonies and sorrows of the worldly matters. This realisation dawns on those people who have opened their heart to unleash the spiritual ecstasy. The experience is so divine and enormous that it is not possible for anyone to put the feelings in human words.

Frequently I have been asked questions about the various techniques of knowing oneself better so that it is possible for a person other than a regular practitioner of spiritualism to understand the intricacies of the spiritual world through simple and affective techniques.

Meditation is one of the most easiest and powerful methods of knowing oneself fully. It is like a flowing river and it is easy to work upon it without the requirement of a guide. Everybody does meditation in its subtlest form in day-to-day life but due to oversight and the fast lifestyle we are living we tend to ignore it. When we enter a new place we try to observe the colours, textures, wall hangings etc. similarly when we meet a new person we observe his body movements. The quantity of observation varies from person to person, but observation is a basis for all the activities in our life. Be it advertising for a product, selling of a concept, convincing a person all requires ample amount of observation and the right attitude for the acceptance of the idea. This type of meditation is working basically on the physical body and conscious brain; it does not work upon the spiritual body. In this book I will be talking of meditation that can help an individual to tap the inner energies and also to unleash the power to help you to work towards the attainment of the spiritual goals.

Meditation is learned easier through a Guru and this book will work like a guru in providing the requisite amount of knowledge and some very powerful meditational techniques to work towards the achievement of the spiritual goal.

It is meditation that provides the practitioner with the insight to the type meditation suitable for him to follow. There can be thousands of meditation techniques but the one that is suitable to a person can only be understood and accepted by a practitioner who derives benefit from it.

This book is meant basically for the beginners who have an interest to know themselves better and also to find a way to get inner peace. The purpose of writing this book was not to fill the beginner with lot of traditional concepts and methodology but to provide practical techniques that can be done without much guidance. By providing the techniques alone it would not suffice for a practitioner to enter the realm of spiritualism. For an individual to get a feeling of the field of spiritualism it is important that the practitioner should have atleast the bare facts for working towards the goals of reaching the ultimate energy.

In this book I have included only those techniques that can be easily done and does not require lot of practice and concentration. Some of the techniques mentioned in this book are so simple that it can be easily done in the office itself.

Even though the techniques look simple but they are as effective as any other advanced levels of Meditational Technique. The Techniques are unique and can be useful for beginner as well as for advanced sadhaka.

Acknowledgements

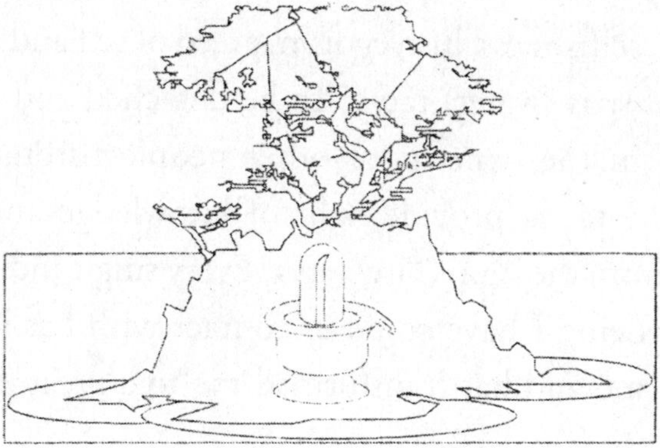

ॐ NAMAH SHIVAYE

Learning is a continuous process, everyday in life provides a new means for learning, and this knowledge has been like a boon provided to me by the Universal Lord himself. Every bit of knowledge provides me with a new teacher and new waves of thoughts develop.

Every single iota in nature has been responsible for the growth and transformation in a simple being like me. The gross body of mine made of the five tatvas, five gyanindriyaes and five karma indriyaes have provided me the starting point of reference for a Guru.

I learnt the concept of accepting pain and doing good to others from the Prithvi (Earth) tatva, cleansing thoughts, selfishness, lust, egoism, greed of self and others from the Apas (water) tatva. To be detached and yet be involved in the benefits of other people through the Vayu (Air) tatva, provide light of knowledge and give warmth from the Agni (Fire) tatva. Every single individual or living being I have come in contact with has left his mark on me and has transformed me to a great extent.

In the physical form I would like to express my eternal indebtedness to my parents, who were the first and foremost teachers in my life. Then I would to like thank my aunties who have loved and cared for me like their own son.

They all provided the base on which my teachers built the humble building of knowledge. With the blessing of God Almighty Aghoree Baba Pinadrik ji, Lama Dzsong Rinponche, Swami Chidanand Maharaj, and Matang Baba who were gracious enough to teach me many ancient sciences that has helped me to present before you my humble work.

My eternal indebtedness lies with all the life forms that have in one way or other have provided me knowledge.

I would also like to thank Mr. Kuldeep Jain and Mr. Ashok Jain and Mr. Shravan Jain for their endeavour to promote a humble author like me and for their encouragement. Thank you Sir.

R.Venu Gopalan
427 Dhruva Apartments
Plot No. 4, I.P Extension
Delhi – 110 092
Email : venrudra@yahoo.com
Website : www.soulsearcher.org

Walking on the air

Floating on the clouds everyday,
I think of the matters of life
Like a bud to be flowered
The essence of life flowing around
Like a bee looking for the nectar
In the hot summer
Songs of life playing a sonata
Telling me I am one of them
Dreaming is not a passion
But an obsession with me.
Living the life of death
But looking at the sunrise
With its every ray touching
My very existence saying
I care for you I am there for you
I pray never to wake from
The dreams of life and happiness

R. Venugopalan, 1995

Contents

Demystifying meditation

Meditation is the most commonly used phrase and yet it is the most difficult terminology in the field of spirituality. Though frequently used it is very difficult to find a comprehensive definition to the word "Meditation". As per dictionary *meditate* means *to reflect upon* or *contemplate*. But this is a short definition of the exhaustive word meditation.

Meditation can be said to be a process of walking on the air. It is a process of reaching towards such depths of consciousness that allows an individual to comprehend the heights of supra-consciousness. The depth of the consciousness is determined by the involvement of the person to the worldly attachments. The more attached a person with the world the more superficially he gets conscious, the lesser attached with the cosmetic nature of the world the higher will be his tuning with the consciousness. This process gets complicated by the process of pain and agony perpetuated by the world. These complications act as a barrier between the common person and the Supreme truth. This restriction works well till the time the search for peace and happiness is outside, but the moment a person delves deep into himself he gains the Supreme Knowledge. This supreme knowledge elevates the person from the superficial strata to the level of conscious understanding.

Meditation is a unique process as more you explore the inner realms the more you are happy and at peace externally. No other process in this world has the power to create such beautiful experience than meditation.

How to really start meditating? Mind the most powerful force in the universe can be programmed and tuned to activate the senses responsible for indulgence in the process of meditation. The mental attitude has to be developed to work upon the ideas in such a manner that it is able to contemplate thought processes.

To explain in simple terms meditation means a continuous process of concentration and de-concentration. In the beginning the practitioner begins by the process of concentration, then the meditation occurs and later the contemplation of the event occurs.

In the beginning the practitioner starts by the process of concentration. But what do we concentrate upon? We will be concentrating on our inner consciousness and the moment we are able to delve deep into the roots of the consciousness we will be provided with a way towards the spiritual or awakened mind. This is the stage of meditation and this when furthers allows the human mind to contemplate upon the various factors of thoughts. It is in the later stages the contemplation of thoughts loses its objective as in the later stages it becomes a stage of thought-less state. This state has been termed by many names like samadhi, the spiritual trance, mystical union filled with the communion of the nature and energy.

We have mentioned that the point of concentration should begin with the inner-consciousness. How can we know if we are concentrating upon the inner consciousness? In the beginning the mind will wander and it does not allow the physical body to control it. So how will we start the process of concentration? Ancient Saints had understood this problem and had provided various means of controlling mind. For any beginner it is necessary to understand that before starting the process of meditation he should be in a position to handle the mind in such a manner which could help him in his endeavour.

This is only possible when the practitioner has enough love and passion for knowing the true knowledge and this love and passion in turn provides patience. This patience provides detachment leading to the stage of pure consciousness.

I can understand that this is not an easy path to follow in the beginning but it is important to have the goal in front before we can actually work towards it.

Sage Patanjali has showed that there are three steps for fulfilling meditation in his Yogasutras.

- **Pratyahara**

  Abstraction or withdrawal of mind from the sensuous objects or attraction to their memory.

- **Dharana**

Concentration

- **Dhyana**

Contemplation- the process of absorption of the feeling of oneness with the ideal

This awareness of calm internal silence has often been confused with the dullness or sleepiness. This awareness is the process of spiritual aspiration and spiritual clarity. This is important for the proper harmony and maintenance of the mind, body and soul. The biggest drawback in meditation is the misconception that it is just related with the mind and the role of body and soul is very miniscule. This myth can easily be dispelled with the following example: during the stage of deep sleep and deep state of meditation the consciousness of the body, mind and all the other elements are dissolved into nothingness and only the soul remains awake without any individuality.

The techniques provided in this book work from the very basic levels and provide a base to reach higher realms of meditative capabilities. This then helps an individual to get rid of complex web of details which he had over loaded himself for many years.

WHY SHOULD MEDITATION BE DONE ?

We have discussed to a great extent about the meaning of meditation but have not delved upon the goals of meditation. This is an important factor as meditation without goal would be like a body without soul, a Rose without its aroma.

(1) Science has proved beyond doubt that meditation can normalise blood pressure, metabolism and to balance of brain hemispheres.

(2) Meditation provides a base for attaining peace with one self and provides for the expansion of inner consciousness. The regular practice helps in the clarity of the mind.

(3) This clarity of mind leads to the cleansing of the body from the negative energies like resentment, hate, prejudice etc.

(4) Meditation helps to energise the body, mind and spirit in such a manner to have a feeling of oneness with the universal energy.

(5) Meditation helps to understand and appreciate the vastness of our being and also to differentiate between the reality and illusion so that the dark shadow of ignorance is dispelled from the mind.

(6) Meditation in general helps to relax, reduce stress, improve health, and to live in harmony.

HOW SHOULD MEDITATION BE DONE?

We live in a world filled with different type of meditations and it will not be possible for a single person to cull the vastness into any particular form. Each of this meditation has its own life and process of death.

Each technique encompasses within itself the whole cycle of life and death.

Birth ← Childhood ← Youth ← Middle Age ← Old Age ← Death

When a person starts to meditate he starts with a dead mind, since he is full of tension, agony and emotional stresses. The release of these stresses from the body life provides the stage of old age. At this stage though the body has released most of the stresses it is the mind that wavers with various thoughts, it requires the experience of a middle aged person to purge them so that mind also could release the varied thought processes. The next stage is the process of reaching inwards to gain strength of youthfulness to break free of the various blockages. By this time you have reached the levels of innocence and the moment you are in the midst of meditation the world vanishes, relatives vanish, friends vanish, and you are alone in the entire cosmos of universal light. This is the place of divine ecstasy, each religion has its own name but the experience remains the same.

The purpose and methodology of doing meditation is to reach the childhood, the divine experience that we have forgotten for so and to becomes a part among us.

As the childhood is very restless thus in the beginning it is quite normal for a person to get tired from the stages of contemplation, thus whenever the mind wavers bring the awareness back to the stage of calmness.

I remember an interesting event that happened at a friend's house. One day we were discussing about the concept of anger, suddenly my friend's youngest son came in and asked, *"What is the difference between anger and exasperation?"* Before I could say something my friend got up and said, come I will practically show the difference. He took the phone and dialled a number and as soon as the line got connected my friend asked *"Could I talk to Hari"*, since the telephone had a speaker phone we heard the other person saying that no such person is available in this number and disconnected. He again dialled the same number and asked for "Hari", this time the person on the other side got bit annoyed and told in a stern voice *"How many times should I tell you that there is no such person called Hari here"*. Third time when he dialed the number the person on the other side started abusing at the top of his voice. My friend's son was about to interrupt, but my friend prevented him and redialed the same number again and as soon as the line got connected he said *"Hello, I am Hari this side. Was there any call for me?"* there was a long pause on the other side before the line got disconnected.

My friend turned to his son and told that in the first case, the person on the other line was disappointed for getting a wrong number second time he got annoyed, third time he became angry and lastly he reached the level of exasperation.

I found the whole event very amusing and very practical. This is also a method used in everyday meditation. The more we tire our mind the better it is, which will provide a way to surpass the consciousness to reach the supra conscious level. We can do a simple experiment to understand this in a better manner.

Sit in a comfortable position and feel the breathe going in and coming out from the body. Stop breathing immediately and close your eyes, for a few seconds you will find that your mind has become blank. The moment body feels the urge for the oxygen it will bring back the awareness to the physical body, and the concentration shifts back to the breathe. The mind however hard you might try will urge to inhale so that oxygen is supplied to the body. Inhale again and repeat the process as given above. You will be surprised to find that after few repetitions the urge for inhalation has reduced.

Similarly in the beginning when a person starts meditation the mind wavers and urges the body to look for other alternates rather than meditation. Practicing meditation regularly will calm the mind to a certain extent.

Meditation is an art that we have been practicing from childhood in one form or the other. When we feel tired we lie down to rest and the body automatically slows down our breathing pattern so that mind and body both feel relaxed.

All these are meditations but the difference is that people only consider structured meditations as meditations. They feel that a person should sit and should be fully aware of the whole process. When we take a walk in the woods won't our mind record our awareness of the walk. It is only the awareness that brings the pleasure, not the walk. Similarly the meditations in this book try to bringout the awareness in a person rather than providing him long talks on meditative philosophy.

WHEN TO DO MEDITATION?

The bestaccepted and suitable time for meditation is Brahamamuhurata (4a.m. - 6a.m.). Brahamamuhurata is the last phase of the night before the dawn. This time is of special importance for the meditators due to following facts:

- The mind is very calm and quiet after a relaxing sleep in the night.
- The mind is like that of a child and thus is nearer to the nature.
- The atmosphere and the environment is very quiet and calm.

But the lifestyles of city does not allow such kind of early waking hence following time can be taken into consideration for doing meditations:

Prime Time	Medium Time	Average Time
4 a.m. – 6a.m. 9 p.m. – 11 p.m.	6 a.m. – 8 a.m. 8 p.m. – 9 p.m.	Before 10 a.m. After 11 p.m.

Average time should be followed only when the other two timings are not suitable. It is advisable to sit twice a day so that the energy is sustained and carried on to the next day. The duration of the sitting can be from 15 minutes to an hour.

Most of the people have holidays on Saturdays and

Sundays and this is a good period for doing meditation. Do rigorous meditation during these days and consume only fruits and milk. The same thing can be formulated on other holidays. As per the seasons, winter is the best time for doing meditation, as it is possible to sit and practice rigorous meditation for longer duration of time.

Some important things to be remembered before delving into the meditation process:

- There should be atleast a gap of two hours between meal and meditation.
- Always do meditation at the same time and same place if possible as the energy will be maximum and will help in providing a faster level of samadhi status.
- Never do meditation when you are emotionally upset, as this will produce negative results.
- The reverence to the master and the universal energy should be encompassing your whole body before you can actually delve deep into the process of meditation.

There are many methods of meditation and whatever technique you adopt should be followed properly before proceeding with other techniques.

WHERE AND HOW TO SIT

In this book I have provided many techniques that does not require sitting at one place. But wherever I have provided such techniques, I have provided a brief about the pattern of sitting required. But in general it is important to know the method used for sitting for meditational purposes.

Sitting forms an important part of meditation as it represents the energy centre for the meditation done. Meditation is best done in peaceful places like on the banks of the rivers, mountains, holy places. Such places have high priority for spiritual development due to their high level of cosmic vibrations. Mostly such places have the kind of environmental setting which provide the required level of temperature, peace and calmness resulting in a practitioner to reach the depths of self-realisation faster.

If the above places are not within the accessible reach then the practitioner should select a clean and comfortable place to sit, which is devoid of noises and sounds. If the meditation is done in a sitting position then sit facing the North, East and West direction.

It would be better to have a separate meditation room, which is not used for anything except for meditation and prayers. This will increase the flow of spiritual energy in the room. If possible adore with pictures of the Lord and spiritual books in the room, light a lamp and incense sticks in the morning as well as evening. After certain period of time this place will emit spiritual vibrations and whenever you feel mentally exhausted sit in this place and you will be surprised to find the quick rejuvenation.

In cities mostly people have small places and it is not possible to have a separate room for meditation. In such cases have a small place like an altar where you should place pictures of the Lord, light a lamp, and incense sticks in the morning and evening; this will be your puja place. While meditating use a meditation mat and use this mat whenever you sit for meditation and if possible sit as near to Puja place. This mat will store some of the spiritual energy emitted by you while doing the meditation and thus it would help you get into the levels of meditation faster and quicker.

If you are not comfortable in sitting on the mat you can place a small cushion on the floor and then sit on it. Even after placing the cushion if you are not comfortable to sit for long hours you can sit on a chair with the feet's firmly placed on a cotton rug. During the process of meditation sit with the spine erect and try to breathe through the stomach. It is important to sit for meditation for at least thirty minutes, if not more.

Never sit on the plain floor for meditation, as the earth will absorb all the energy generated through the process of meditation. Always use thick cotton mats or woolen mats that are easily available for meditation.

❋❋❋

Postures

If we look at the ancient sculptures of Mojen-jo-Daro and Harappa, we find that many of the sculptures are in the Lotus postures. This is so done to show that the capabilities of the posture. These postures are very important for a person moving into the realm of meditation.

IMPORTANCE OF MEDITATION POSTURE

For any meditation process to be successful it is important to bear in mind the following points:

- The posture should allow the practitioner to remain aware and alert.
- The moment the posture becomes uncomfortable the concentration of the practitioner diverts itself from the ecstatic state of meditation to the discomfort.
- Never lie down for doing dhyana as this leads automatically to a deep state of meditation rather than a better level of concentration.

SELECTING A POSTURE

Most of the ancient people in the field of meditation talk about sitting postures like Padmasana, Siddhasana etc. These postures are effective to people who are flexible and have had long hours of practice. Even in India people living in cities cannot sit cross-legged on the floors for hours.

Thus it becomes necessary to sit in a posture that is comfortable to the body. In this section I have covered various types of postures and methods of sitting for the benefit of the practitioner to select from.

VARIOUS MEDITATION POSTURES

Sitting Posture in a Chair

People living on cities are most comfortable in this posture as nearly half of the time we spend our time sitting on a chair. For a beginner this is a perfect method of sitting for meditation.

For doing meditation sitting on a chair the following things are to be kept in mind:

- The back should not touch the chair. Only the base of the spine should touch the chair.

- The spine should be kept erect during the whole process of meditation.
- Place the palms on the knees facing downwards. The feet should be firmly placed on the floor.

POSTURE WITH A CUSHION

Though we feel comfortable sitting on a chair, the actual level of satisfaction derived by sitting on the floor can never be achieved. If sitting cross-legged on the floor is difficult, a firm and comfortable cushion can be used for sitting.

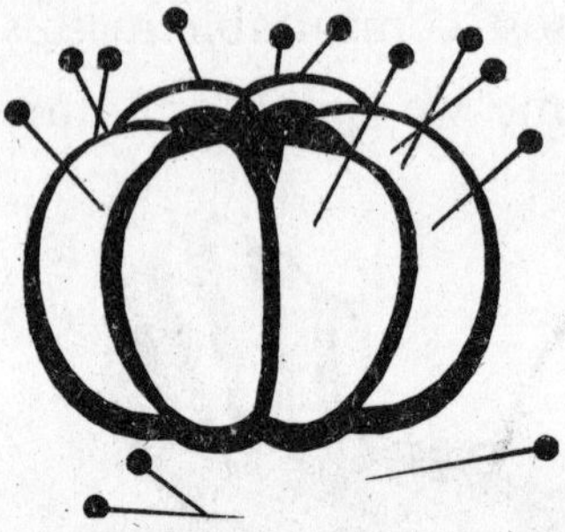

Zafus or Meditation cushions are now available in India, earlier they used to be imported from various parts of the world. These cushions are designed in such a manner that the meditator is able to derive maximum benefit during the process or ritual.

There are different postures for sitting with a cushion:

- **Two Cushions are better than one:** In this posture one cushion is first placed on the floor. Stand at the end of the cushion and kneel over it (Buttocks will be touching the ankles). In such case the cushion will be comfortably placed between the ankle and the knee. Take the second cushion and place it between the calf and the thigh region. Some people feel comfortable with one cushion.
- **Cross-legged on a Cushion:** The description of the cross-legged postures has been provided in the coming pages. The difference is that a meditator will sit on a cushion with the cross-legged posture.
- **Multiple cushion posture:** In this case a meditator uses multiple cushions for getting a stable posture. For example in beginning if a beginner sits cross-legged on a cushion then it is quite possible that after a short time the knees may start aching. Thin cushions placed under the knee will provide the support to the spine as well as the posture.

TRADITIONAL POSTURES

The Yogic tradition follows a method that is suitable for the people who are into the practice of Yogic Kriyas, asanas and Bandhanas. These postures require the body to be flexible and supple.

Warning!!!! - People who have any medical problems should do these asanas only after consulting with a medical expert.

Some Important instructions:

- Never force yourself in a cross-legged posture as this can cause damage to the joint bones and muscle.
- Forcing oneself in a posture that is not comfortable cannot provide the required solace in achieving meditation comfortably.

Pathetic cry of a father heard in a jail during the meeting time with his son

"I am fed up with you: attempted robbery, attempted burglary, attempted murder, attempted assassination, attempted suicide.

You are a total FAILURE CAN'T YOU SUCCEED IN ANYTHING YOU TRY OUT."

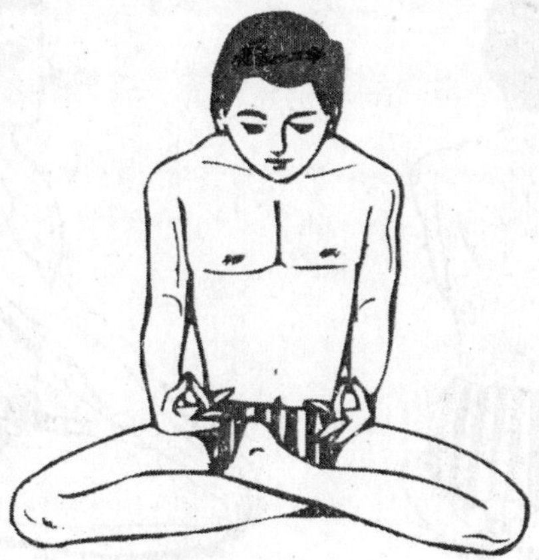

GUPTASANA
(The Seat of Ecstasy)

Sit with the legs stretched out. Bend the right leg placing the heel against the pubic bone. When you feel comfortable in this position then bend the left leg in such a way that the left heel is above the right heel. In such a case both the feet are near to the pubic bone providing no pressure on the perineum. Place both your palms on the knees or near the pelvic bone.

Master is one who stays back, he is the divine force who is far ahead of everything else. The reason for his growth is that he has recognised that he is not among so many illusions.

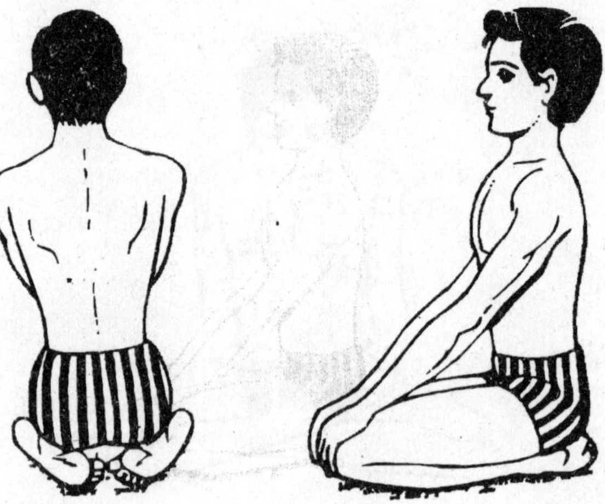

VAJRASANA
(Posture of Thunderbolt)

Stand straight keeping both the feet together for doing this asana. Bend knees and sit upon the heels. Both the heels of the feet should form a 'V' shape for allowing the buttocks to rest comfortably on them. The knees should be kept together and the spine should be erect with the hands resting on the knees.

Divine love is when two entities merge to form one, it is not physical but divine ecstasy is the downpour of the pure energy. Let go of your consciousness and you will find the eternal divine door of the love.

SUKHASANA
(Easy Posture)

Sit on the floor with stretched out feet. Bend the left foot and place under the right thigh. Now bend the right foot and place under the left thigh. Keep your spine straight and make sure that both the heels of the legs are touching the ground. Place both your palms on the knees.

This is Sukhasana because it is very easy to sit on this posture and also a beginner should start with this posture as it helps him to sit in advanced stages of asana.

SIDDHASANA
(Posture of the Master)

Sit on the floor with stretched out feet. Bend the left foot and place the heel of the foot at the perineum. Adjust the left foot in such a way that the pressure is felt in the pubic area. When you feel comfortable in the position, bend the right foot over the left foot, in such a way that the right ankle is directly above the left ankle. Push the sole of the right foot in the left calf. Keep the spine erect and shoulders should also be kept broad.

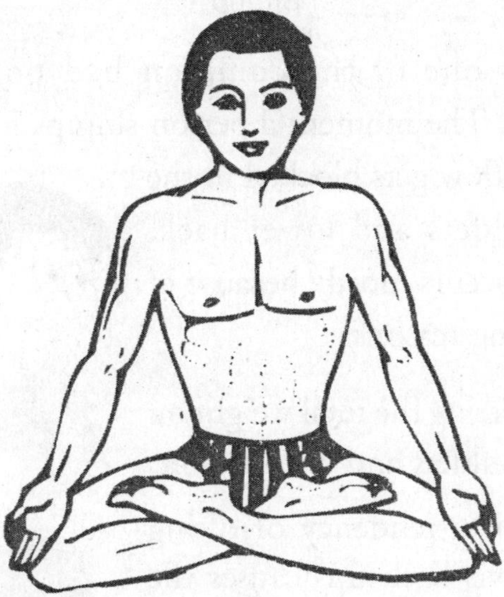

PADMASANA
(Lotus Posture- The most stable posture for meditation)

Sit on the floor with stretched feet. Bend the left foot and place the left ankle over the right thigh (sole facing upwards). Now bend the right foot over the left thigh, in such a way that the sole faces upward. Make sure that the sole are as close to the hip joints as possible. Place both the hands on the knee and assume the posture of gyana mudra with the palms facing upwards. Keep the spine erect and shoulders wide. This posture is called as padmasana because when a person sits in this posture he looks as if he is sitting on a lotus.

BAD POSTURE
Slump

This is one of the common bad postures for meditation. The moment a person slumps in a posture the energy flow gets blocked in the neck shoulders and lower back. Slumping occurs mostly because of the following reasons:

- Transferring the total weight on the shoulders and neck region.
- There is a tendency of tilting the pelvis back this causes the front body to slump to provide the required support.
- Forcing yourself to sit in an erect manner causes undue pressure on the spinal column causing the body to bend forward to balance.
- Slumping can cause the following problems to the meditator
- Slumping causes the chest to shrink causing lesser intake and transfer of oxygen.
- Due to lesser transfer of oxygen the body tends to get dull and it is quite possible that the meditator falls asleep.

There is another posture that is equally damaging to the meditation; this is when a person forces himself to sit erect. Puting pressure to sit erect causes the body to curve backwards. This arching of the body could damage the condition of meditator as the throat gets dried as well as cause sprain in the neck.

GOOD MEDITATION POSTURE

For understanding the details of a good posture it is important to first understand the effect of various body parts while posturing.

Head

When you sit for meditation the most important part of the body that is to be taken into consideration is the head. The head should be in the centre of the shoulder that is to say that the head should be in alignment with the spinal column.

Neck

The neck should be erect with relaxed feeling surging at the back of the neck. Touching the tip of the chin to the throat can easily do this.

Never force your chin to touch the throat region as this can create dullness and it is possible that the meditator can fall asleep.

Spinal Column

The spinal column should be straight so that the energy can flow smoothly. A person is said to be sitting straight - only when the spine makes shape of 'S'. The shape of the spine should be similar to the diagram provided.

The moment posture become perfect the wandering of mind stops and allows the practitioner to develop the inner awareness to a great extent.

Shoulders

After adjusting the head and neck it is important that the shoulders are also kept in a proper position for getting the maximum benefit from meditation.

The shoulder plates should be straight and the chest area should be open. This will provide the free flow of the breathe in and around the body. This can be easily done by doing some quick inhalation and exhalation while concentrating on the chest region.

Hands

The important factor is to understand the placement of hands. If the hands are not placed properly then the whole body gets disbalanced and it may not be possible to develop concentration.

The most appropriate place for keeping the hands during the whole process of meditation is on the knees or near the navel centre. The important posture for the hands is the Gyana Mudra (the posture of knowledge). For achieving this posture touch the tip of the index finger with the thumb and place the hands on the knees facing upwards.

In India, ascetics use Dhand (a wooden curved arm rest) for doing meditation this helps in balancing the body as well as controlling the flow of energy in a systematic manner. If it is not possible to then place a cushion on your lap and place your hands over it.

Buttocks

This is the most important part of the body that comes in contact with the seat on which you are sitting be it floor or chair.

If the buttocks are not firmly on the seat of meditation the practitioner will not feel grounded and it is quite possible that the wandering of mind becomes uncontrollable.

Legs

For any posture to be successful it is important that the grounding is perfect. This happens only when the placement of the legs is done properly. In traditional posture the body is locked in such a manner that legs automatically reach the designated posture. In the other postures it is important that the legs are comfortably placed. If the practitioner uses a chair then it is important that the legs donot cross each other at the level of the ankles.

Some important points to be kept in mind:

- There should not be any strain in the thighs, calf and hip region. This is important as strain causes the mind to be in the state of consciousness.
- People with medical problems should consult doctors before doing traditional postures.

❋❋❋

Food and meditation

Food plays an important role in the meditation process and it is important to follow certain rules for getting success in meditation.

- Never sit for meditation after a heavy meal.
- If possible avoid non-vegetarian foods, as this will help releasing the excess heat from the body. If it is

not possible to avoid non-vegetarian food then eat it sparsely (once in a week to once in a month)

- As far as possible avoid oily, fried and spicy food.
- Consume as little tea and coffee as possible.
- Take as much as liquid diet as possible, this will quench the requirement of hard food.
- More will be covered in the following pages.

Meditation and self-descipline

The physical body is made of carefully inter related webs of atoms and molecules that allow the energy to flow through our body in a systematic manner. This interrelated physical form also represents the external manifestation of the inner energy (Soul).

Meditation is an interrelated process of mind and

body, the first step is relaxing the body, thereby stilling the mind. The moment mind gets stilled the pathway to the universal energy opens providing unlimited source of energy and power to the practitioner.

The major purpose of meditation is to do self-purification. Many people claim that they can bring drastic changes in other people but actually it is the perseverance and endeavour of each individual that provides the basis for the development and changes.

More and more a person works on the process of meditation the higher and higher he reaches the inner consciousness. In scientific terms if we explain then in a normally awakened person the brain waves work at the rate of 13-40 Hz. At this level we are able to concentrate, focus and are fully in the consciousness. This level is called the BETA level of awareness. The moment the brainwaves are reduced to 7-12 Hz, we reach a level of relaxation, creative visualisation. This level is reached when we work on something that is very close to our heart. A person at this level is aware about the people around, but he is not influenced by them. This level is called the ALPHA level. Hypnotist uses this level for programming the mind and also for retrieving the information from the sub-conscious mind.

The deeper a person reaches inside himself the brain waves also slow down to 4-7 Hz. At this level the individual is able to tap the memory store bank and retrieve the information therein. Dreams, vivid visual images are seen at this level. This state happens when a person is at the verge of deep sleep. This state of brain waves is called THETA level.

The brain reaches the final level of intimate knowledge when it reaches a wavelength of 0-4 Hz. This state is known as DELTA level or a stage of deep sleep. At this level the mind and soul gets separated from the body and a feeling or detachment occurs. This level is called the Samadhi level where one is having a fully matured detached awareness.

Thus it is important for every person desirous of getting into the realm of meditation to develop the will to work seriously and observe discipline.

This book has been divided into various sections and each section is like a small workshop on meditation, by the time a person completes the book, he should have done at least a course on meditation.

The meditation techniques provided are simple yet powerful so it is my sincerest request that people who want to benefit from meditation should follow each of the techniques in sequence as this will help in building a strong base for development. Continuity of the meditation practice in seclusion of the mind is the secret of the technique's success.

Most of the meditations have been provided with their own rules and precautions, which are provided keeping the practical aspect of mind. These rules are created based on experiences of meditators trained over the years and are both scientific and rational.

This book will act as a guide and a Guru for those people desirous of knowing more about meditations and this will become a reality only when the person doing this course understands the relevance and importance of this whole course.

CODE OF DISCIPLINE

The practitioner should try to follow the discipline codes for getting success in the techniques provided in the book.

- During the period of doing this course, the

practitioner should be willing to comply fully with the guidance and instructions as given in the book without ignoring any part, nor adding anything to them. This acceptance is required, as the attitude of trust will help the practitioner to work regularly and thoroughly. This trust also helps the technique to provide the success in the process of meditation.

- Do not try to mix any other meditation techniques with the techniques provided in this course.
- No drugs, alcohol, or other intoxicants (tranquilizers, sleeping pills) should be taken during the whole course.
- Medication due to medical problems can be continued.

❋❋❋

LOVER OF YOGA

Once a great Bat researcher reached a humid, moist and dark cave. Inside he found thousands of bats. He was very much thrilled at such a great opportunity. During his search for more bats he saw a Bat standing upright on the floor. Upon asking the Bat, the Bat replied he was an avid lover of Yoga and he is doing a Shirsasana (headstand).

Important facts before starting this divine journey

For understanding any science it is important that rules pertaining to it are also followed so that it is easy to cross the hurdles that might creep up during the journey. I remember an old story that will prove the point clearly.

In an ashram there were many students and it was a ritualistic practice of the ashram to attach newly initiated disciple with two or three old disciples for growth of understanding and creating harmonious situation where everybody could gain something new every day.

One day the Swamiji asked a newly initiated disciple to go with two students to meditate near the riverbank. All the three reached near the riverbank and sat to meditate. Suddenly one of the elder students stood up and said, "I have forgotten my meditation mat. You two continue, I will get the mat and come back soon"

Saying this he took the first step into the water and miraculously walked on the water to reach the small hut on the other side. He went inside and got the mat and walked across the river and sat down to meditate. The whole episode was so miraculous that the new disciple was dumbstruck.

The moment the older student sat down, the second student got up and said "Swamiji had asked me to cook the rice for the ashram today, wait I will return in a moment after putting the rice for cooking"

Saying this he also walked across the river and after some time he came back and sat down for meditation.

The newly inducted student felt that this is something miraculous and Swamiji might have sent me along with these two old able students so that I could get this siddhi.

Since he had observed the other two students walk across the river, he also stood up and said-"Thanks, I think I have learnt this great siddhi (mastery of a technique) from both of you and let me do this, so that you both could tell Swamiji about a fast learner like me".

Before the other two students could say anything, the new student took the first step and plunged deep into the water. He came out undeterred and tried again, but without success. He kept on trying for sometime and lastly came out exhausted, and started weeping.

The two students who had watched his efforts to walk on the river with great interest came near the new student and slowly said in the ear of the student.

"We have no siddhies as you thought, we have kept stones in the river bed and we had been walking over them which you never knew"

Just to avoid hurdles, I will be explaining the basics for each meditation in detail and as a beginner you should go through the theoretical part thoroughly before starting any of these techniques.

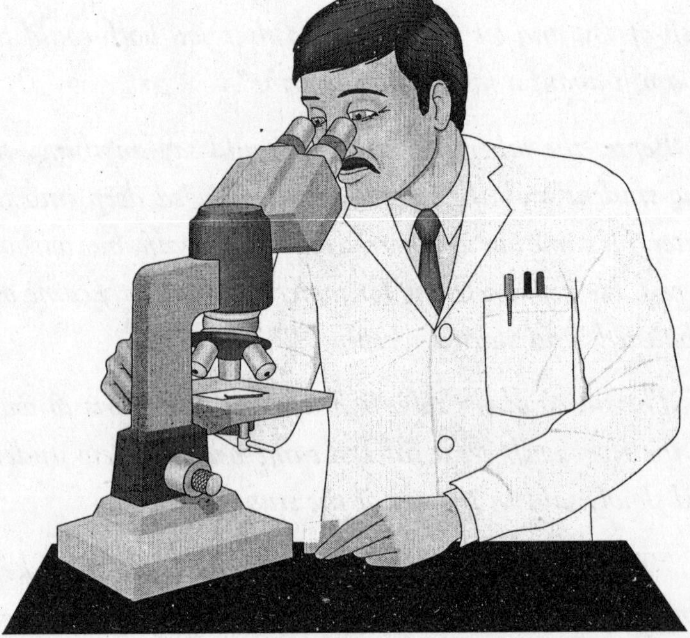

Word of advice

- Meditation is a spiritual process and those people who believe that it is sort of mental hocuspocus, should not tread on this path.
- Since meditation provides lot of variations in the thoughts of the practitioner only a person who believes that it is not difficult to detach from the worldly beliefs, faiths, relations etc. can reach the very heights of this divine blessings.
- Never hurry yourself to learn all the process at once, as this will prove dangerous. When a child learns to walk he is clumsy and it is a big effort on the part of the child to keep the steps in a proper manner,

similarly a practitioner should follow each step with caution and should proceed only after achieving success in one process.

- Success in a process is said to be achieved when the mind is controlled and works as per the requirement, then only the desired results will come.
- Mind is controlled when the doubts and unwanted thoughts are cleared when only it is possible to reach the depths of meditations.
- Meditation is a process of creating a sense of ultra-awareness. The moment a person is able to perfect the meditation he is aware of everything yet not involved in any of the activity surrounding him.
- Never be disheartened with failures, as failures are actually the achievement to the goals partially. You should restart from the stage of failure to find the goal faster.
- Advanced practitioners should read a lot instead of meeting unwanted people, if they want to achieve the state of samadhi.

Obstacles in meditation

- The most powerful obstruction in meditation is the Laziness. This is the reason why most of the practitioners of meditation leave the spiritual experience as quickly as they have started with the practice. This laziness is caused by many factors like over stuffing your stomach with food, over work in offices and lack of time due to travel and societal commitments.
- While doing meditation the second largest distraction is the **hordes of relatives, friends and well-wishers.** This can be avoided by having a process of detachment with the relatives during the process of meditation. Detachment here does not mean avoiding their closeness, but to be attached with the supreme at all periods of time.

- **Sex** is the next biggest obstacle in the process of meditation. Sex has been the reason for the failure of the most of the practitioners of meditation. These thoughts can be avoided by trying to follow a path of little rest, chant and meditation. Regular brisk walking for half an hour is best exercise for diverting the mind.
- **Disease** creates a feeling of indifference in the mind. This indifference leads to a process of doubts, suspicion, and drowsiness. During the period of disease the best method of meditation is chanting and meditation processes that require active participation rather than passive participation.
- **Forcing** though process in mind to work according to a certain pattern can create more hassles and a sense of disillusionment. This can be handled by allowing the thoughts to tire themselves out so that it is easier to control or to divert the thought to such an extent that it automatically comes under your own control.

❋❋❋

A world of meditation

MY FIRST STEP TOWARDS MEDITATION

Modern world is a world of constant changes. If we compare it with the lifestyle prevalent during the pre-modern era the changes are enormous. In this modern era if we adapt and include simple things in our life style, it can help to discover ourselves faster. For doing these types of meditations and to derive benefits you do not require to follow strict pattern of postures or any other forms of restriction. The pattern of meditations described in this section is based more on the concept of KARMA theory.

Karma means action, any action that has some relevance to our life is called Karma. Another definition of Karma is that of one's alliance to duty, this duty is not just restricted to the official work only.

Karma theory is not just related with the past deeds done by us, which has a wider impact on the life, but it is also relevant to the day-to-day activity undertaken by us. There are thousands of activities that form a major part of our daily life. These activities combined together form a reason for providing changes in ones life.

HOW THESE MEDIATIONS WILL AFFECT THE LIFESTYLE?

These meditations will work in the following manner:

- In the beginning, it will start with providing a base for self-awareness.
- In the next stage the self-awareness spreads through the physical and ethric body.
- The conscious mind starts in conjunction with the sub-consciousness and supra-consciousness.

Though the meditations that have been covered in this section cannot be called as a true meditation process but helpful for an individual to get into the roots of his own self. This then helps an individual to gain more insights in the lifestyles of other people and thus helping him to understand the intricate web of true and happy living.

Benefits of doing these meditations

- These meditations will provide a clearer conceptualised thinking process.
- It will also bring in the method of living in a community.

Daily Meditation Series #1

NO MASS MEDIA

The all-encompassing arena of Media surrounds the lifestyle of an average city dweller. Media be it Radio, Television, Cable, Internet, Cellphones, Newspapers etc. have bombarded our lives in many ways.

In cities an average person spends more than 6 hours in front of the television and more than four hours listening to radio, reading and surfing the net. The extent of impact of the media can be judged from the fact that the fictitious characters in the serials have started forming a part of our lives.

I have seen people discussing the characters of the soap operas as living beings. The extent to which we have been affected by the soap operas can be gauged by the hue and cry made by people when the role of a character in one of the famous serials was cut short. Such kind of imaginary lifestyle has taken its toll on the people's psyche. They have started leading a life of dreamland woven by the media barons.

Such a lifestyle not only damages the physical but also the psychic aspect of the living.

The purpose of doing this meditation is to bring back the lost levels of awareness. This meditation does not require a person to sit but it is just a game of will power and you will find a new self that which is glowing with the energy of the universal self.

Remove yourself from the gamut of media for few days in the beginning. This will look difficult in the beginning but after few days you will find a new pattern in your life.

How can you remove yourself from the over powering effects of the media? The simplest way is to divert your attention to a particular hobby or a longing desire. This hobby will gradually transform internally in such a manner that after a certain period of time you will hardly find time to get entangled in the cosmetic web of the media.

I have seen the exceptional changes in people who have diverted their attention from the add-on complexities of the media. They have become better people to deal with and their thinking and lifestyle have also become more sensible. Such people have a better sleep compared to people who get infused with the media.

BENEFITS OF DOING THIS EXERCISE OUTWEIGHS THE ADVANTAGES OF MEDIA:

- You will be able to free yourself from the varied cosmetic experiences of the serials
- The concept of media is centered on the concept of Attention Interest Desire Action. Media catches

attention of the viewer/reader through an interesting article/ program and later a desire comes into the mind of the viewer/ reader to adapt some of the policies into one's own life, thereby taking action. What is actually happening is that the program/ article converts your individual persona into the persona of the author of the program/article. The moment you disseminate from the artificial environment you will find more space inside yourself as you are away from all the different personalities you got inspired over the period time.

- Since the media relies on the concept of suspense, drama and intriguing plot, sooner or later it causes the mind of the viewer to get inquisitive about the programs.
- The dream patterns change from the time you disseminate yourself from the media.
- The power of imagination and visualisation will improve and develop your ESP.

- If the spare time is utilised for the benefit of other fellow person then the inner satisfaction is also achieved.

Daily Meditation Series #2

WORK FOR LIVING & NOT LIVE FOR WORK

In city life the average time spent on job is about 8-9 hours forming around 56-63 hours a week. This is a major part of life that is being spent to earn a livelihood. For a person who wants to develop spiritually and live normally it is important that the individual is able to cut down the working hours.

Actual requirement of life is simple and can be achieved within a period, but when we run after the mundane accessories then more time is wasted on such activities. I remember an old story that goes a long way in explaining things in a new light.

A Sadhu lived in a small hut in a jungle. He used to take his bathe in the river, eat fruits from the jungle and spend the rest of the day through meditaton. One day while gathering fruits, he found a goat. He felt pity on the goat and brought it along with him. In the morning as usual when he got up he got worried as to what will he give to the goat for eating. He immediately went out in the jungle and gathered some fresh leaves and shrubs. By the time he came back it was noon. Few days later the goat gave birth. Sadhu consumed a portion of the milk and sold the excess milk to the villagers. As time passed, he brought a cow and recruited a servant to sell the milk. As the business flourished he got married and settled down.

CAN YOU FIND SOME SIMILARITY BETWEEN THE STORY AND OUR LIFE?

When a person starts working the income is less and so are the needs but as the income increases the needs also increase. This is a vicious cycle of finance and needs and this cycle that forces an individual for doing more hard work and still the satisfaction level is never reached.

The nature has particular rhythmic clockwork that has survived for time immemorial. Birds, animals, plants and humans all work in the similar pattern of lifestyle. Look at the nature around all the animals and birds strive for their survival. When their stomach is filled they come back to their homes and donot strive till the next day. This has been going from time immemorial without any change; but only humans have changed the nature according to their needs . Humans are the only animals who even after having reached the optimal level of consumption tries to snatch the consumption material from other fellow human beings.

Reduce the time spent in the office and you will have sufficient time for developing your energy and to lead an exciting and interesting life without harming any other living organism.

Daily Meditation Series #3

COOKING A MEAL

Food is one of the most essential parts of life and yet very few of us like cooking. Cooking as such is a beautiful art. I always believed that preparing the meal is very similar to the preparation of a portrait by an artist or writing a book.

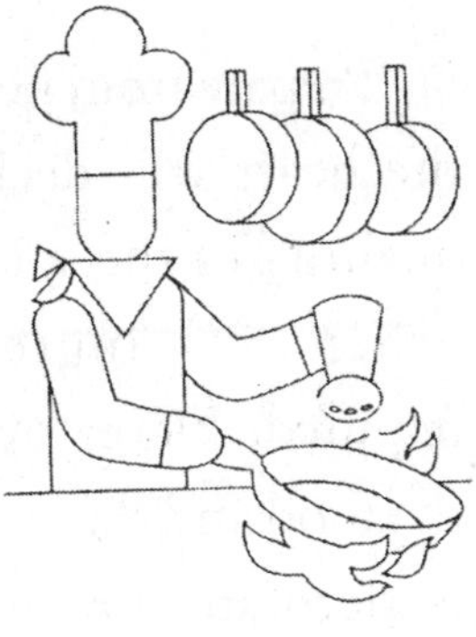

You need not prepare a lavish meal but even if a simple meal is cooked with love and affection will provide the happiness you have missed for long.

Prepare the meal and share it with your family or friends. After the meal extend your services to the washing and drying of the dishes also.

The secret of cooking a dish starts from the stage of selection of raw vegetables, spices etc.

Cutting of the vegetable also requires the creativity, each piece should have the distinct flavour of your touch and the feeling should flow from your heart. It is important to savour the smell of all the raw vegetables and other spices while cooking the food.

Prepare from heart and the heart will decide the quantity of the spices and other ingredients required. Never overcook the food and do not forget to decorate the dish with mint leaves, chillies, tomato slice, lemon slice etc. as per the requirement.

Serving the food is also an art. The meal should be started in a group so that the feeling of oneness is there.

Never be in a rush to finish off the meal, relish the dish while talking and unfolding all the good old memories.

You will not believe it but by the time meal is over the feeling of fulfillment is not just with the stomach but also with the heart. Even while washing or drying the dishes do it in a group to create togetherness among people and also provide a time for chatting and joking .

After the meals, provide some sweets or coffee/Tea etc and enjoy in conversation which will help in the digestion process as well as to know each other better.

Daily Meditation Series #4

THE ART OF FOOD TNTAKE

Life without food is like a body without blood. From ancient times man has been struggling all through his life for satisfying his hunger.

Every Christian asks for bread from Jesus after the prayer and not the wealth of the world. Food obtained from different sources has different energies and in order to avoid the negative energies of food, it is important to energise the food with positive energy.

This being an active meditation, it does not require the practitioner to close his eyes.

When the food is served touch the edge of the plate and say the prayer in the following manner

I am thankful to the Universal Energy I am thankful to the hundreds of people who have strived hard for providing me this food Let this food provide me with energy and other nutrients for survival, health and vibrant life.

Touch the food on the plate and pray to the lord for providing positive energy to the food.

Eat slowly and let the juice of the food get mixed with your saliva. Feel that with each bite the energy is flowing into your body.

Remember to say the Lords name with every bite of food. After finishing the food touch the plate again, say the prayer again, and mentally bow to the plate.

This process of eating food will result in better absorption and assimilation of the food in the stomach.

Tip:

Before and after the meals touch the heart also with the left hand and pray for the fulfillment of the life force.

Daily Meditation Series #5

RELATIONSHIPS

This is another important feature in our life that has been ignored by most of us. Previously the relationship and togetherness was important but the self-centered western influence has forced many of us to lead nuclear families. This change had severe impact on the psychology and vulnerability among the family. Children got affected most, as they do not find elders to guide them.

India was popular for the joint family system till few years back but the impact of western influence coupled with greed for material gains and disrespect for elders completely destroyed the joint family system and paved way to nuclear family comprising husband, wife and children. Children were under the mercy of servants and crèche.

In a joint family there were more than twenty or thirty people under one roof, with clearly defined daily work routine for each individual. The hierarchy was clearly defined and bonding was done with the help of Grandparents. This bonding was so strong that every decision was taken collectively resulting in harmony in the household. The income and expenses were shared equally, profit distributed equally thus creating a congenial atmosphere in the house.

This system survived for many centuries as each and every individual felt that he is part and parcel of the family and owes a responsibility to the family. But the industrialisation changed all that and now we have developed the concept of individualisation. Every modern individual believes that what he thinks is perfectly right and any interference in that is dealt with severely. The goal and aim of the individual is restricted to himself and rarely include the members of the family including the parents.

As in the western world this attitude is also clearly visible in Indian cities, and when the child reaches the age of 18 he starts his life as per his own conditions and the role of parents becomes non-existent. This has resulted in creating a vicious circle of victimisation of the individual roles in comparison to the collective roles. The child will pass the same kind of callous attitude to his children and the process will continue to alienate a person from the parents from the childhood.

I remember a colleague of mine, who though born in an orthodox family got alienated from his parents due to their busy schedule. He was always insecure and afraid of every thing he did. He used to hide everything from his parents and got furious when some matters came to parents knowledge.

He had many short love affairs before he had secured a respectable job. Since the job required him to be away from his own place of residence, he got relief from the eyes of parents for a considerable time. After a year or so he opted for a live-in relationship with girl in his office and the parents were hurt by his attitude. But they could not interfere with the relationship, as by now their own child was unknown and stranger to them. The pain and agony in the eyes of the father was visible but it was too late to bring back his son.

The above is a true story and is happening day in day out in the world of today. The alienation is not restricted to parent child relationship in a nuclear family but also between the husband and wife. The alienation between husband and wife is so high due to self-ego, career prospects, financial strength, extra-marital affairs, material benefits and commercialisation of each facet of life which strains the relationship to the extent of breaking. It is very common how to see people holding many degrees and high positions opting for divorces. It is amusing to read in papers that the divorces are happening on petty grounds like the sound of snoring, body smell, sweaty body, inability to cook, losing temper etc.

We have actually lost sight of the nature of humans, the attitude we follow is worse than that of an animal. We abuse people by calling them by various names of animals like Gadha (Donkey) but have we ever given the thought that our nature is worse than that of these animals. These animals have not lost their attitude but we have lost all our culture within a short span of few decades.

The level of openness among the family is important to a great extent for bringing back the trust of the family members.

I remember the incident narrated to me by an elderly person that relationship with family is like a gardener to his saplings. When the gardener brings a small sapling he plants it in a small pot and cares for it like a mother to a child. As the sapling grows the gardener changes the pot according to the plant's size, and cares for the plant like a father and this goes on till the plant reaches a certain level after which it is not possible to keep the plant in a pot any longer. The gardener takes out the plant and plants in the earth and cares for the plant like a friend.

In the same way the change in relationship should happen in the family. A child should be loved, cared, looked after till the child is not in a position to control his own emotional aspirations and as soon as he grows up he should be treated like a friend, philosopher and guide. The moment we are able to establish this kind of relationship, the child will feel open towards the family and the secrets would be shared among the family.

The understanding of the parents would pave way for the future planning of the child and this understanding is possible as the experiences are the same only the constituents change.

The lifestyle and living pattern of the parents reflects the child's growth and it is possible to guide the children correctly so as to avoid being tempted by the same kind of experiences that their parents went through. The most powerful tool in the world called love easily achieves this. Love brings forth the powerful stimuli that merges the body together in such a way that only the soul is visible and the physical body loses its physicality.

Love is not physical but it transcends the realm of physical realm to reach the spiritual levels. On the physical level when love is shared it is joining of the bodies that can be separated, but the actual love is one where physicality loses its importance. Though a child and mother are physically separate but the moment a child comes running and hugs the mother, the physical bodies merge to form a divine energy. This happens because love demands

nothing and it is pure acceptance and understanding. The moment this flow of energy is achieved the dark aspects of deceit and secrecy loses its entity and is bathed in the cosmic energy of love.

TWO IMPORTANT THINGS THAT IF AVOIDED CAN HELP YOU TO CHANGE INDIVIDUALLY

I have often seen people washing dirty linen about their family members in public this happens due to two important factors - firstly they have not accepted the family secondly they are hesitant to accept their role in keeping the family intact. This leads to their role as a family breaker in the long run.

The second group of people loves to criticize and make fun of others, but the moment somebody talks about their family they get irritated as if hiding secrets. This does not symbolise love for the family, as a person who loves ones own family loves other's family also.

The concept of "Vasudeva Kutumbakam" represented love for everyone and in such cases there are no secrets. Stop looking at others, they have the same kind happiness, sadness, problems like you have, so the moment you remove all your sadness, problems, others will also be relived of the burden.

Through this meditation the major highlighted fact is to start spending more time with your family and you would discover a new experience engulfing your whole entity.

Start taking interest in the daily life of the children, grown ups and parents so that they have the feeling of oneness. Every single activity becomes a part of your life.

This can be easily done if the life is lived fully. The meaning of living fully means, in the office spend time as an employee and when at home spend time as a part of the family. If the attitude of office is carried back to home then there would not be any difference between an employee and a member of the family.

There are two types of people in this world one is extrovert and the other is introvert. An extrovert is the one whose physical eyes are open while the introvert is the one whose inner eyes are open.

An introvert becomes successful because he is always in the process of perfecting his thoughts while an extrovert moves with the thoughts.

Just before meditation

BODY TALK

For getting success in any technique it is important to have a strong base on which we can fully rely upon. The most powerful and strong equipment we posses from our birth is our body. Body is one thing that we can trust if we have actually worked towards knowing our body well. This section will provide you a basis for understanding the energy that resides in our body and the methodology

for de-stressing yourself in such a manner that you become mentally, physically and spiritually prepared for the Divine course in Meditation.

The tensions and stresses that occur during the day is taken in stride by the individuals because they get stored as reserves in various parts of the body. We will be talking about the important parts where the stress gets stored and also provide techniques for releasing them.

FACE

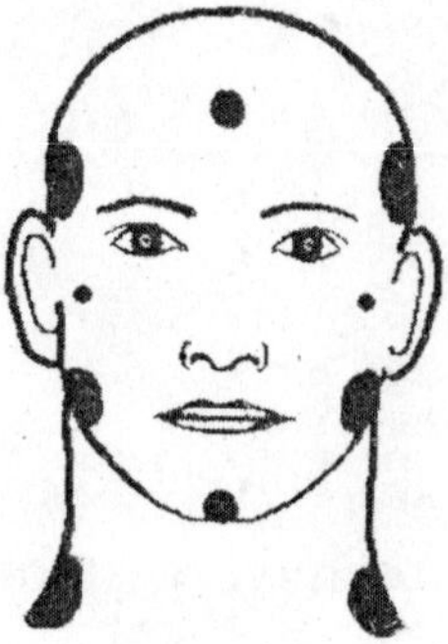

This is the most important part of the human anatomy. It is important for two reasons - one it is the first part of the body that is seen by people around and secondly it is the body part that has three major senses of the body viz: eyes (for seeing), ears (for hearing), nose (for breathing).

Stress and tension get stored in the face faster than in any part of the body. The diagram of the face has been marked with ten half circles, these ten half-circles represent the centres of storehouse of stresses and tension. These tensions and stresses grow over a period of time and cause various diseases like migraine, Blood Pressure, Heart problems etc.

CHEST

This is the second major region where the stresses and tension have huge storehouses. The sternum region is the fascinating region that provides the basis for knowing if a person is undergoing stressful atmosphere.

The more a person is under stress the more will be expansion of the sternum region. This happens to act as a protective shield for the heart. It also helps to build up of ego, selfishness and other negative thoughts.

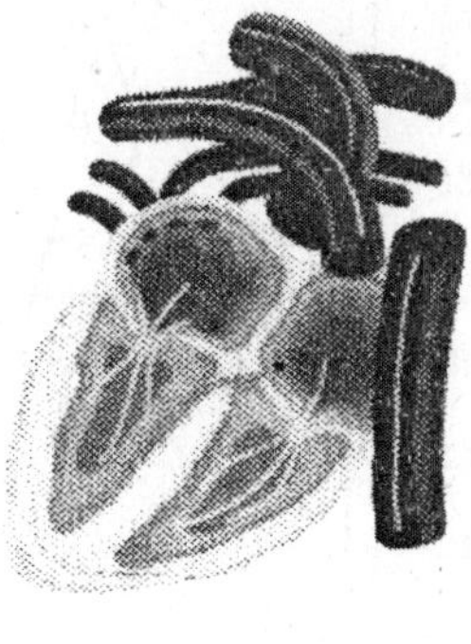

How can you find on your own that there is piling up of stresses in sternum region? Simply stand in front of a mirror and place both your hands on the sternum region. Breathe in and out deeply till you get the feel of the movement of the sternum region. Now gently push your hands inwards and release. If the sternum moves in with the pressure from hands and gets released with the release of the hands then your stress level is under control. If not then you should look in the De-stressing techniques.

STOMACH

AGAR PETH NA HOTA TO KUCH NA HOTA

(If there was no stomach then nothing would exist)

The above Hindi sentence aptly says it all. If the body did not have stomach then there was no problem at all. Hunger is the main cause for all that happenings in this world. But hunger has to be understood deeply before saying something on this aspect. The world suffers from two different types of hunger, one that is natural and the

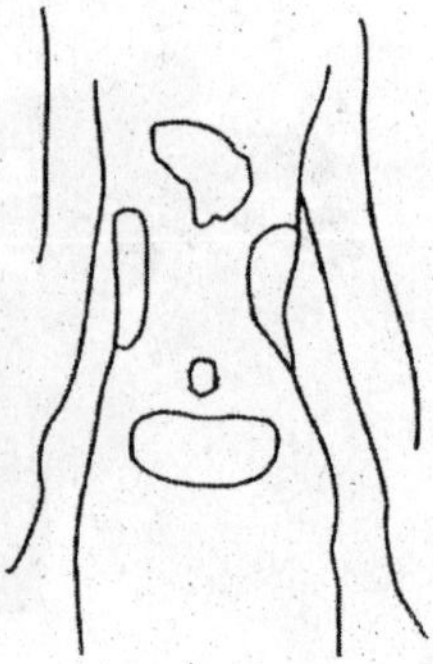

other is created and unnatural. The former is something that is one is born with, and the latter is attribution of the society and the wrong education, which developed the unnatural hunger.

Shaded portion shows the places where the stress and strain gets stored.

This unnatural hunger in the form of wealth, ego, status, anger, hatred, envy has led to the development of strains and stresses in the relationships. All these have attributed to the development of gas troubles, excess development of bile juice, diabetic.problems etc.

SPINAL & LOWER PARTS OF THE BODY

Passion is the most negative aspect that causes the major setback in the field of meditation. This passion is found in the curve of the back.

In the diagram the position of the passion has been shaded. For

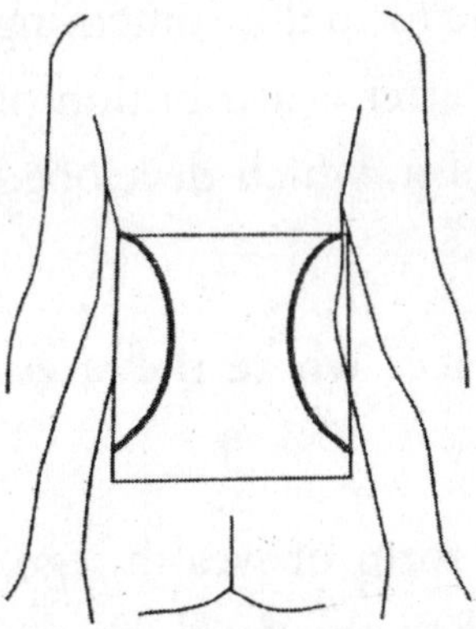

a controlled level of passion the curve is normal. If the body has a deep curve (represented by the black curve) or straight curve (represented by the gray box) it will definitely block the flow of the passion resulting in building up of frustration and depression. The lower part of the region of hip joint is also the centre for proper growth of passion.

DE-STRESSING BODY

In the above discussion related with body parts we have found that today a person is under more stress and strain than any time.

This section is a process of de-stressing that will allow you to release the strains and tensions from various parts of the body so that you are totally fit for the meditation in a natural manner.

Note: All the de-stress exercises are to be done for five minutes each and should continue till the pain vanishes. This process can be done with partners also, as it will be easy for them.

DE-STRESSING FACIAL CENTRES

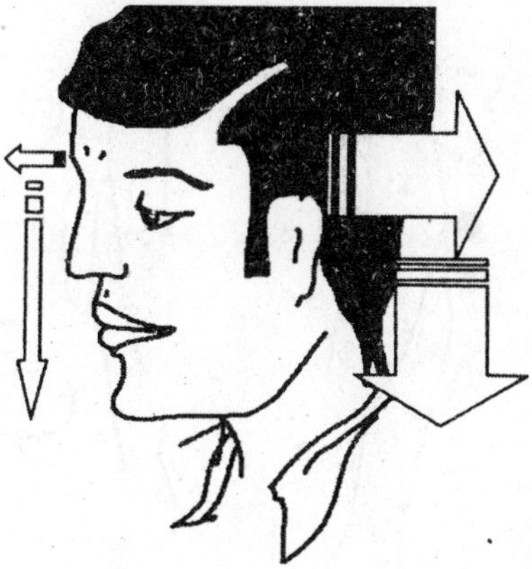

The simplest process for de-stressing the face is to partly open the mouth, let the tongue touch the upper palette and move your head either back towards the spinal column or towards the chin. During the process keep breathing normally. This technique is very effective when a person is undergoing through stressful moments or emotional upheavals.

Second method is to cover the face with both the palms and watch the fingertips with slow breathing process.

DE-STRESSING THE CHEST, SPINAL AND STOMACH REGION

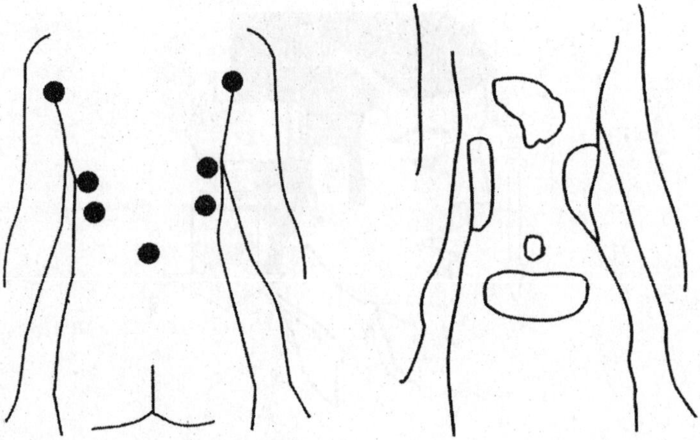

Use the thumb of both the hands to press gently on the shaded parts of the chest and stomach. It will pain but ignore the pain and continue doing it. It is quite possible that you will yell at certain points and would scream at others but the pressure should not be reduced, as it is a process of releasing of all the stored negative energies.

DE-STRESSING THE PELVIC, HIP AND FEET AREA

This part of the body requires an important de-stressing activity more than any other part of the body. The pressure areas are near the tailbone, cavity of the hip joints (represented by a dark circle in the diagram), inner and outer thigh region.

The process of de-stressing starts with the pressure being applied to the tailbone by the thumb. The up and down movement of the thumb on the tailbone will release the agonising emotional upheaval. If you want to cry loud do so, as it will help you feel lighter and better.

The main reason for the release of such huge amount of emotions is due to the fact when a person is emotionally distressed he tightens his thighs and tries to bring the knee nearer to his chest. This he does so that the thighs act like and armour to the body. The pelvic region closes in such a manner that the person feels a surge of energy through his body. This is the energy flow that connects humans to the earth.

Practitioners should follow the methods provided in the same chronological order for getting maximum benefit from the de-stressing process.

Regular practice of the de-stressing methods will make you ready for the meditations that have been covered in the following chapters.

The next chapter also provides more methods for the process of de-stressing.

DE-STRESSED NOW WHAT?

Some points are to be kept in mind after the process of de-stressing is done, and one of the major factors is that you should not allow the stress to creep back.

- Start loving yourself. But make sure you donot become a narcissist in the process.
- Never let the judgement of others affect you. How should it be done? Every day before going to sleep say "I thank the Universal Energy for creating me in such a unique and wonderful manner. He has left the faults in me so that the ego does not overcome me from doing the assigned task". Repeat this every

night and you will see the difference.

- Accept that you have faults and are in a process of learning till your death. This will open your avenues greatly as you will learn from every moment of life. This can easily be done with the power of observation. Observe every incident of life be it small or big but never get involved in the process of observation.
- Be regular in your meditation practice and you will find that stresses and strains will never come anywhere near you.

❋❋❋

> Master is one who stays back, he is the divine force who is far ahead of everything else. The reason for his growth is that he has recognised that he is not among so many illusions.

Walk thy way into meditation

WALK TO KNOW THYSELF

Remember when the child took his first step. Did'nt it give a cry of triump and success. This first step itself dawns in a new era of learning and experiments. The natural instincts guide an individual to develop and harness each and every bit of knowledge that he can grasp. This is the main reason that when a child starts to crawl or walk he is inquisitive about every single object.

This inquisitiveness is destroyed by the societal pressures and the child is forced to lock all his creative abilities in the form of a revolt. This revolt is represented by undue anger, tantrums etc. When the child grows up all the blockages start to affect his personality in such a manner that he becomes a depressed, frustrated and lonely person.

Many couples come to me for an answer to their unhappiness saying that even after several years of marriage they feel that they were leading a life of a solitude. On further enquiry the most common problem that I have found is that in the beginning the life goes smoothly due to the excitement of change in social status, security feeling , sex and children etc but as the time passes the blockages come in front of them and they feel that they have led a life as per the instructions of the society and not as per their own independent natural instincts. This leads to anger and resulting in arguments and fights.

SOME OF THE BASIC QUESTIONS REGARDING WALKING-MEDITATION ANSWERED

How to resolve the problem?

First Walk in the human life has caused this problem to develop and grow. So it is important that we start the process again from the stage from where we stopped in the first place.

Walking though a physical exercise will get transformed into a process of divine meditation by the time you reach the end of this section.

How will a physical exercise resolve blockages?

Walking is a process that has been done by us from the childhood. We will be taking your experience of walking as a booster for the meditation to happen. Walking when done with a focused mind transforms the physical exercise into a process for the release of the blockages.

The techniques provided in this section will prove a basis for the expansion of the power of observation- both self as well as external.

It is said that in meditation you have to withdraw and close you eyes. How is it possible to say walking is meditation?

There are lot of differences between walking meditation and sitting meditation. In sitting meditation the method is to withdraw from the external world so as to reach the depths of your own soul, this will become clear from the section on sitting meditations.

In normal walking a person only observe about the surroundings, while in walking meditation you become an observer. The observer is working at two levels-The physical level the observer is protecting from all the hinderances and on the awareness level the observer will delve deeper into the inner realm of mind and soul.

Will I be able to do the meditations with walking?

The techniques provided in this book are not meant to scare people away from the realm of meditation, but to bring them to a new level of awareness.

Walking has been taken as a method of providing a better understanding of meditation, the main reason being that every individual has the knowledge of walking. The new lession you will learn new is the process of creating self-awareness while walking. The moment you have mastered one form of walking you will be able to pick other forms easily.

You will not believe but is true that a person becomes more aware when he is in the process of motion. In stationary meditation process the mind becomes active and in active meditation the mind becomes passive. Thus, it is possible to learn the meditation faster in a process of motion.

Wouldn't the process of walking become monotonous after mastering the process?

No. As you will see that there are many techniques in this section that will really provide you an exciting journey into the new realm of walking. Walking itself will become a new habit to people.

When should Walking meditation be done?

Any time of the day is suitable for walking meditation. Even short trips can become walking meditation if done properly. Some of the techniques require specific period of time that have been explained in the technique section itself.

Walking meditation is not suitable if done in summer afternoons, as it will drain out the strength and lessen the awareness levels.

How should Walking meditation be done?

The process of walking meditation is not difficult as it involves only bringing the awareness to the walk.

THE BEGINNING

What is the first thing a child does when he stands up for the first time. He takes the first step you might say, but it is not true as the child first tries to stabalise himself then only he will begin the first step.

Moving Meditation #1

STANDING ALONE

We will start from the very basics, even though you might have had long experience of walking for hours together.

Forget the styles of walking followed by you. Just start afresh but the experience of yours will guide to work towards the goal in a better manner.

The first step is to just stand.

How to Stand?

Stand means to stand with awareness. This awareness involves knowing your posture, weight and subtle movements of various parts of the body.

While standing put your arms on the sides of the body loosely, have a gap of five-six inches between the feet and keep the shoulder, chin and face straight.

The weight should be equally divided between both feet. You can do this by first leaning on the left feet, feel the strain, then lean on the right feet , feel the strain and then straighten up both the feet till you feel the entire body weight is divided equally between both feet.

Touch the navel with the palm tips of both the hands and breathe in deeply. Hold the breathe and release slowly.

Repeat the process of slow deep inhalation and exhalation for five times, this will make you aware of the centering of the stomach as well as its strain limits.

Note: Do not move any other part of the body while doing the deep inhalation and exhalation process.

While doing the deep inhalation and exhalation bring the awareness first to the stomach then to the chest and lastly to the movements of the palm. You will be surprised to find that your upper body parts, shoulder, chest, stomach and arms will also move rhythemically in tune with the breathing pattern.

Stay in this divine state for five minutes. This technique will generate awareness about your subtle physical body, if done regularly.

Moving Meditation #2

FLEXIBLE NECK

Neck is the most vital part in the human body that shows the flexibility of the spine. If the neck is stiff or tight then it is important to let the blockages get released from it so that the walking meditation becomes a pleasure rather than a pain taking endeavour.

For doing the *Moving Meditation #1- Standing Alone* first then bring back the hands on the sides of the body and start breathing normally.

STEP 1-I AM A GOOD WIPER

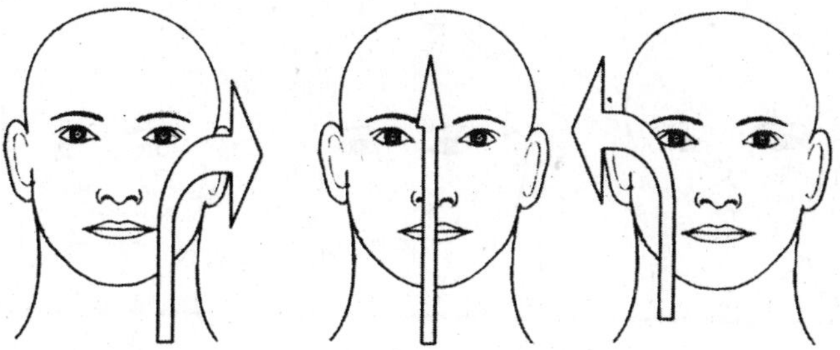

Keeping other parts of the body straight move only the head towards the left shoulder as far as possible, count slowly to 10. Bring the head back in the centre and stay there for a slow count of 10. Move the head towards the right shoulder as far as possible and hold for a count of 10. From a distance, if looked , it would look like a moving wiper.

During the whole movement breathe normally and whenever you feel strain or pain stop and rest.

STEP 2-SWING ON

Keeping other parts of the body straight move only the head towards the chin as far as possible, count slowly to 10.

Bring the head back in the centre and stay there for a slow count of 10.

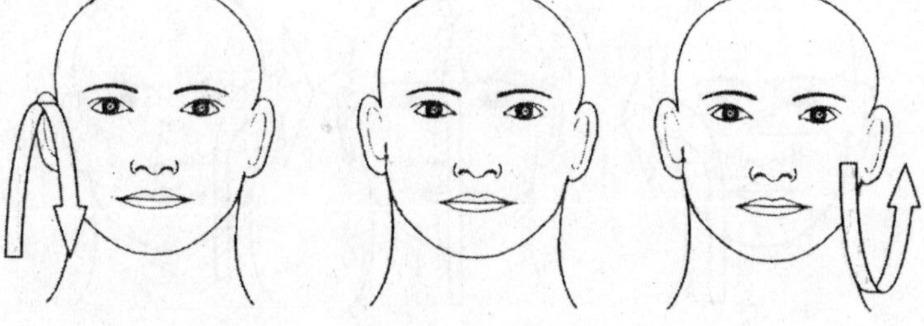

Move the head back as far as possible and hold for a count of 10.

During the whole movement breathe normally and whenever you feel strain or pain stop and rest.

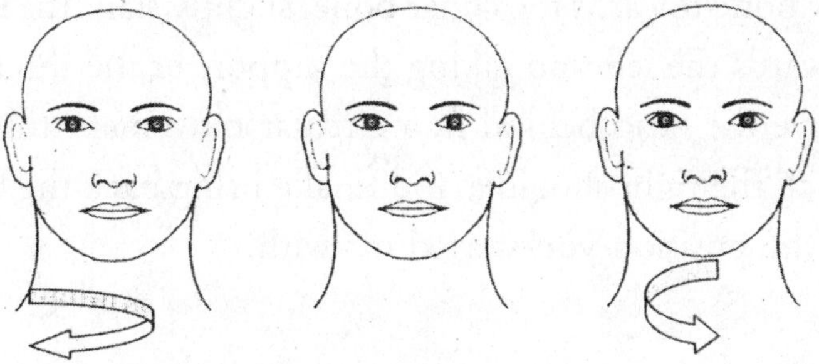

STEP 3- TWISTING COLUMN

Keeping other parts of the body straight bend the face towards the left shoulder as far as possible, count slowly to 10.

Bring the head back in the centre and stay there for a slow count of 10.

Bend the face towards the right shoulder as far as possible and hold for a count of 10.

This exercise will release the blockages stored in the neck region.

STEP 4- ROLLER COASTER

Keeping other parts of the body straight move only the head in anti-clockwise direction. Slowly lower the jaw bone towards the collar bone, slightly slant the head towards the left and taking the support of the shoulder move the head behind in a circular movement till you reach the right shoulder and finally bring back the head to the position you started off with.

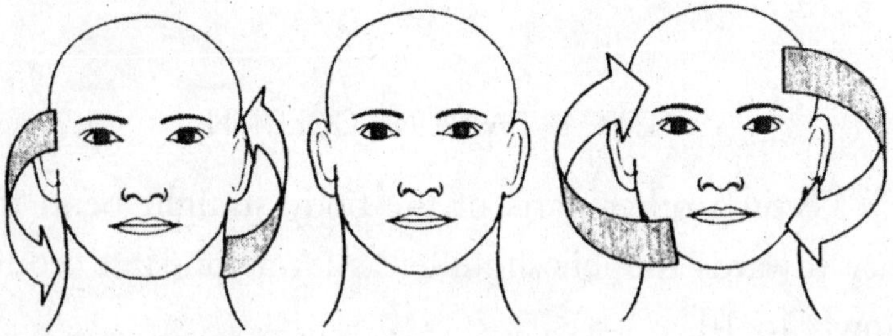

Hold the breath while doing the circular motion. Start brething normally when you come back to the normal position.

Repeat the procedure mentioned now in the clockwise direction.

After doing all the four steps stand still for five minutes and move.

Moving Meditation Series #3

STEP BY STEP

This is a powerful technique for understanding the subtle feelings that get merged with the gross body. Walking is an art and a person who has achieved success in mastering this knowledge can easily master various techniques of meditations covered in this book.

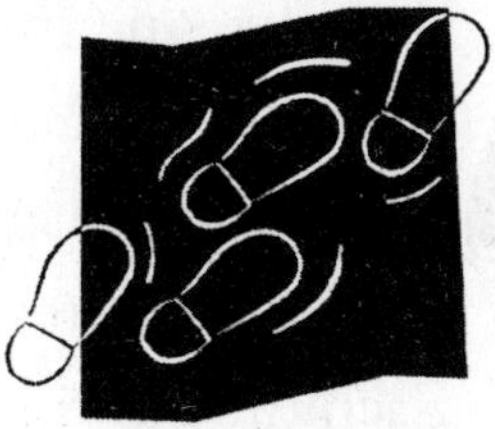

This technique is covered in five steps, taking a person from the base levels of understanding to the higher realms of spirituality. For doing this mediation it is important to wear comfortable clothing and to have relaxed mind.

The first step can also be done indoors and for better results change the place of walk after some time.

FIRST STEP

The first step in any direction is the most important and can change the course of one's life. The methodology to be taken by the meditator is to stand in one place erect with the hands loosely on the sides. Inhale and exhale deeply ten fifteen times. Each time during the inhalation feel the flow of prana spreading throughout the body and during the exhalation feel the expulsion of the residues from the body.

Watch the path on which you have to start the process of walking. Observe the intricate details of the path like growth of grass on the sides, bushes on the edges of the path, the uneven surface, trees etc. The observation should be intense and should allow the brain to store the whole picture of the land on which you will be treading.

1. Raise the first foot slightly and observe the movement of muscles in the hip, thigh, and calf

region. Also observe the movement of the ankles and feet. See the objects under the feet.

2. Move the arm on the same side of foot slightly and observe the movement of muscles while rising of the arm.

3. Now move the foot to the position of the first step and observe the place on which the foot is kept. Move the arm back to its natural position and raise the other arm.

4. Repeat the above steps with the other foot.

This is the technique of doing *First Step*. It is a slow walk process requiring continuous and unabated attention on the path of walking.

Benefits of this Meditation

- The power of observation will increase
- The knowledge of physical anatomy will improve drastically.
- Better coordination between the parts of the body.
- One develops a sense of fullness and oneness after the success in this meditative exercise.

SECOND STEP

This technique should only be done after mastering the first step, as it will provide the practitioner with sufficient understanding of the physical self.

Second step provides the knowledge of the ethric body and how this has been a part of us with or without our knowledge. Ethric body is the cosmic body that is the double size of our physical body. It is not easy do feel and know the ethric body in the beginning so we will begin with some techniques for getting a feel of the thing we can actually see in SHADOW.

This technique is preferably done after sunrise and before the sunset as during this period the shadow is visible and follows the physical body. The methodology is to observe the movement of the shadow with every movement of the physical body. The pattern of walking will be similar to the earlier step and the only difference is the observation will be more on the shadow rather than the physical self.

This is the technique of doing *Second Step*. It is a slow and quite exhaustive walking process requiring continuous and unabated attention on both the shadow and the methodology of walking.

Benefits of this Meditation

- The intuitive development occurs with regular practice of this exercise
- The knowledge of shadow will improve drastically and continuous practice leads to the knowledge of ethric body.
- Shadow walking is a powerful methodology to understand the outside forces acting on our body.
- The knowledge of breathing and flow of breath is understood clearly to a great extent over a period of time.

THIRD STEP

Third step provides the knowledge of external factors that move around us. This technique is normally done in parks or other places where people come for morning walks, running etc.

In this technique the methodology is small yet difficult to follow. The method is to observe simultaneous walking of self as well as of the other walkers in the similar manner as done in the First Step. Continue to do this technique till you are able to observe both yourself and other person fully. Then follow the Second Step with simultaneous observation.

Benefits of this Meditation

- This develops the energy centres and also develops the intuitive capabilities of the practitioner.
- The practitioner is able to develop a keen sense of observation with regular practice of this technique.

FOURTH STEP

This technique should be done after mastering the earlier three steps. The main reason for this is that in the earlier steps we were concentrating upon the physical and shadow aspects of the body, while in this technique we will be working on the visualisation aspect of the walking.

In the beginning do the *First Step* but in this case you will not observe the physical body but the observation will be through the visualisation method. Whenever you take a step, you should have a clear picture of yourself taking the steps and the image should synchronise with the actual physical movement.

Once you have mastered the physical movement through the process of visualisation, do the *Second Step*, by visualising the movements of the Shadow in the mind itself. Repeat the *Third Step* after gaining confidence in the Second Step through the simultaneous visualisation of the walk of self and other person.

Benefits of this Meditation

- This develops the energy centres and also intuitive capabilities in the practitioner.
- The practitioner develops a sense of understanding of the surroundings without getting involved in the situation.
- This technique also provides healers with an opportunity to develop their skills in *Distant healing*.

FIFTH STEP

In this technique no walking is involved but this technique can be done while sitting in one place and can get the same benefit to the practitioner.

In this step the practitioner has to do the *Fourth Step* without moving any part of the body. It will be totally a visual walk.

Benefits of this Meditation

- The power of visualisation develops to its maximum by doing this technique.
- The energy centres opens up very fast with this technique.

Fourth and Fifth Step can be done at any period of day.

Note: Please donot jump steps, as this will not provide the benefits you would like to derive from the meditation process of "Step by Step"

Moving Meditation Series #4

SILENT WALKING

Life from the beginning till death is filled with sounds and noises. The main reason for the sound is to hide the actual inner voice that has a subtle nature. Whenever we are silent the inner voice calls out which provides us with subtle energies that helps out physical Aura.

In the **First Step** we have been endowed with the power of observation and through this meditation we will be blessed with the power of understanding our own energy.

The methodology of silent walking is similar to that of **First Step** except that there is no observation of outer things, nor the movement of muscles of the body.

The observation will be there but it will be for understanding the inner voice.

The technique of doing this meditation

- During the whole process of silent walk concentrate on the breathe. Each individual inhalation and exhalation should be observed carefully as also the flow of energy from the external body to the inner body.
- Feel the breathe flowing down from the throat region to the lungs and from there getting mixed with the pure blood to reach the heart.

Continuously observe this phenomenon with every step taken.

BENEFITS OF THIS MEDITATION

- This meditation will develop the sensitiveness of the ethric body.

- The intuitive power also develops very fast.

Moving Meditation Series #5

BREATHING CYCLE MEDITATION

This unique meditational exercise helps you to understand and tap the energy reservoir in the subtle body and also provides the basis for the development of correct flow of energy in and around the body.

I had covered lot of meditational technique based upon the breathing in *"Soul Searchers- The Art of Breathing"*. The difference between the meditation covered in my earlier book and these are that they were based upon the concept of visualisation while these are active meditations.

Some important instructions before doing this meditational exercise :

- Donot do this meditation after drinking lot of water as it can cause cramps in the stomach.

- People having stomach and heart problems should consult a medical practitioner before doing this technique
- Never do this technique under emotional stress as it will cause more negative energy to flow thus causing more damages than the benefits.

PROCESS OF DOING THIS MEDITATION

Since this technique requires lot of physical movement, the best way to do this exercise is to stand with your feet at the levels of the shoulder width. The arms should be relaxed and should be on the side of the body. Fill your mouth with air and release the air with full strength for five or six times. This will loosen up the body so that all the tensions in the body are released to make you more comfortable and relaxed.

STEP #1

This step is the beginning of Breathing Cycle Meditation, during this process of this technique the breathing will be done through nose.

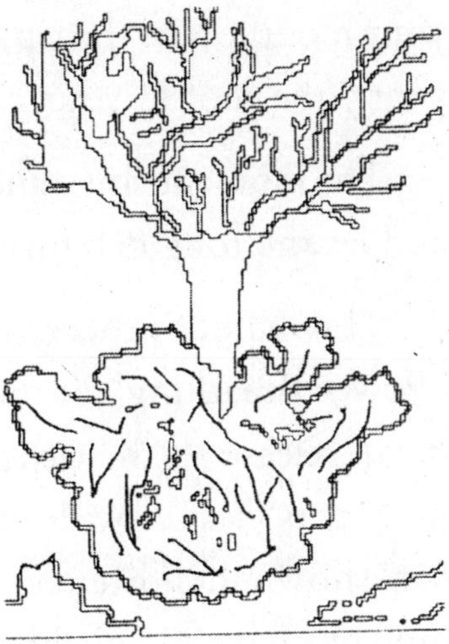

Breathe out forcefully through nose so that all the air from the lower lung to the upper lung is released.

After you have released all the air from the lungs inhale slowly so that the air fills the lower lungs first, then the middle and the upper lungs is filled with the air.

When you feel that the whole lungs are filled with air hold the breath and close your eyes concentrating on the lungs area.

Now, while taking your next breath, focus on drawing into your body an ethric force of energy, which shall flow from the ground and wrap itself around your body. Remember to exhale from the "bottom-up" of your lungs. As you exhale, focus on commanding this energy to remove itself from your body and return to the earth. Remember to breath in from the top to the bottom of your lungs.

Now, do exactly as described above, but breath in first from your nose, with your mouth closed. Inside your mouth, take the tip of your tongue and let it touch gently the roof of your mouth behind your front teeth.

The moment you want to exhale part your lips slightly and let the tongue return to its natural position.

This whole process of breathing is termed as the "**Power Breathing**"; if done with utmost concentration it can release all the toxic waste in the body so that the body gets cleaner with every attempt. Regular practice has shown heightened level of emotional setup in individuals practicing this unique technique. Some people get afraid of the burst of energy in the beginning but as time moves, the energy balances itself with the body rhythm. This burst of energy has been termed under many names some call it the prana, Ki, chi, Odic force etc. Even with so many names nature provides the same kind of experience to every individuals.

This beautiful and powerful technique I have learnt from children who used to cycle near my residence. The way of breathing is unique when a person is cycling, the reason for which is that while cycling the concentration of the individual is on two aspects one on the road and the other on the breath. If he loses concentration on one aspect the control is lost. Similarly a practitioner who is not able to grow past this technique will not be able to do the next level of technique that is the actual Breathing Cycle Meditation.

PROCESS OF DOING BREATHING CYCLE MEDITATION

Repeat the process as mentioned earlier for ten times. Stop, hold and nourish the experience of the unique power.

When you feel that you are ready for this step release all the energy stored up in the body in quick succession. How would you do it?

The process of releasing the energy is to do the process of reverse flow of energy. Spread your hands on the sides Feel that the head of yours is like the roots of a tree, hold the breath, and concentrate on the third eye.

The whole purpose of doing this dhyana is to unwind yourself to reveal the most beautiful creation in the world called humans. Repeat the process of reverse energy flow but now concentrate on the lower abdomen region (Tip: the hairline between the navel and the genital area). In the first case the intuitive capabilities increase while in the latter the centering of the body occurs.

Remember that this technique provides energy when required for recharging and donot use this energy unnecessarily for healing or curing others otherwise your energy will start depleting.

Benefits of this Meditation

- This meditation technique provides instant energy whenever required.
- It helps in strengthening the abdominal region and also the shoulders
- Regular practice will provide insight to the shorter technique that automatically dawns upon you.

Moving Meditation Series #6

WATCHER WALKING

One day two friends met near a shopping mall after a long period of time. One of the friends asked the other "You must have come for shopping? But I see you have purchased nothing till now?"

The other said "No, my shopping for the day is over, I

have purchased as well as eaten nearly everything in this mall. Now I am full and must leave."

The friend looked perplexed, then smiled and said, "window-shopping".

This is one of the most wonderful experiences as we all must have done the window-shopping at one period or another, but this technique will provide a new method of doing window-shopping.

For doing this technique the best way is not to carry any cash or credit cards while going for shopping.

After reaching the biggest shopping market in your locality, do the following steps one by one and feel the enjoyment sweeping through you.

STEP 1

Stand at the entrance of the shop, and observe the door for a minute and the various decorations on the door.

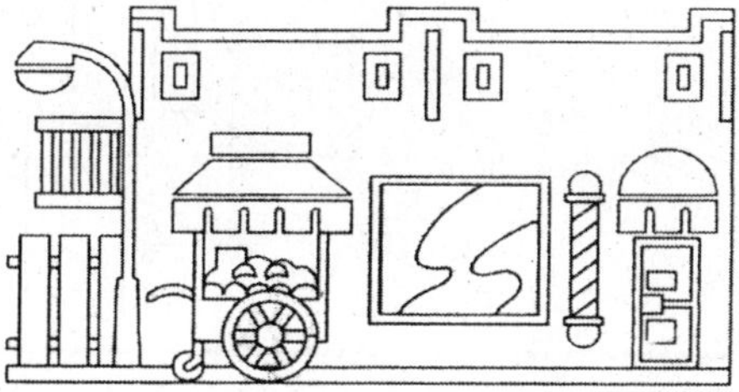

Take the first step inside the door and observe every single item therein. It is quite possible to find a salesperson come upto you asking for any help, observe the salesperson also.

Roam around the store watch and observe every single object stacked in the various shelves of the shop.

The aim of this roaming is not only to roam around the store but also to trace the steps either through a counting system or mental observation. If after fifteen steps and there is a turn observe the turn.

After roaming the whole shop come back to the place from where you started. This completes the step 1 of this meditation.

STEP #2

In this step you will retrace the steps in the same manner as done in the first step, the only difference will be that you will not observe the rows of things loaded on the shopping rack but recollect the things that are stacked on the rows of rack.

This is a beautiful meditation that works on two levels - one at the recollection level providing the person with the knowledge of recollection and secondly helps in developing concentration while retrieving the steps.

This meditation can be done at various places, bookstores, big departmental stores, shopping complexes and large market places.

Happy Window Shopping

❋❋❋

> God loves to joke. Look around in your life as well as others. Every moment provides you an opportunity to laugh at the antics they do you. A serious person cannot be spiritual, only a person who can laugh at himself first then at others can be called spiritual. Spirituality is life and life is fun.

Spiritual meditations

Spiritual Meditation Series #1

DEITY MEDITATION

Have you seen a musician playing the instrument? Firstly he checks the musical instrument properly either by tightening the strings or powdering the moulded leather on the drum before the start of the program.

The moment he starts playing he closes his eyes and the symphony flows through him. For the audience he is just a musician who is playing but for the musician it is a dance of devotion and sacrifice. If the musician is seriously engrossed in the music the tears of ecstasy flow from both the audience and musician.

In the same way, the devotee should fill his heart with love and compassion only then the Lord will grant him the blessings. It is said that before a person knows the Lord he should know himself.

FOR IDOL WORSHIPPERS

Sit before the idol of the Lord. Relax each part of your body and be in a position for receiving the blessing of the Lord. When we talk of position for receiving the blessing then we mean that you have purified yourself to such an extent that the body becomes good and pure vessel for the blessing.

The Physical Form of Lord -Watch the form of the Lord with all its intricacies. Look at the holy feet of the Lord how beautiful they look, the place where they stand. Move from the feet to the calf muscles of the Lord see how they uphold the strength of the universe within themselves. From the calf muscles move to the thigh

muscles, the gracious forms of them enticing you. From the thigh muscles move towards the reproduction area feel the formation and destruction of world through them. Move upto the slender waist of the Lord upon which the land of jewels exists. Move to the heart area, which is ever flowing with love and compassion for every one in this world. The broad shoulders of the Lord guides us to overcome the burden of the karmas. The arms of the Lord ever open to bless and to take the burden from you. Throat of the Lord representing the oceans of the world, which is ever flowing with their silent waves singing a Lullaby for you to get engrossed into. The lips of the Lord represent the happiness and tranquillity of spiritual bliss. The nose of the Lord representing the ladder of growth of spirituality and discarding the material wants. The ears of the Lord representing the patience of the Lord to listen to all your worries and happiness as a friend. The lotus eyes of the Lord representing the three phases of Life- the past, present and the future. The eyebrows representing the futility of the time lapse as created by the human mind. The wide forehead of the Lord represents the all-encompassing nature of truth and knowledge.

CLOTHES & ORNAMENTS

After watching, the physical forms of the Lord observe the clothes and ornaments worn by the Lord. Every detail of the clothes and ornaments should be properly observed so that a wave of sound becomes a symphony.

Close your eyes and recollect each feature of the Lord with all the ornaments and clothes as you have watched with open eyes. Continue doing this process till you achieve a level of perfection in the visualisation of the deity. Bow down to the Lord as from now when you think of the Lord, Lord will be there to protect you.

Spiritual Meditation Series #2

ADVANCE STAGE OF DEITY MEDITATION

Does the Lord exist only in the idols created by humans or is it all-encompassing and all-loving. Generally a person develops only when he comes out of the shell of idol worship and starts seeing and thinking that all the creations and surroundings is nothing but a part of the Lord himself.

He is the owner of the Land, Sea, Oceans, Rivers,
Sky, Humans and anything that exist in the whole
of the cosmos. It is by his wish birth, death takes
places,
and without his wish, nothing happens.

If the above is true why not meditate on the universe itself with all the things in it. Sit in a comfortable position with clear and open mind. See all the things in the room be it the photographs, calendars, chandeliers or anything.

Try to visualise the grace of Lord on that (if you are a idol worshipper then visualise the idol in them). Feel the energy of the Lord in your house, in all the living beings in the house. Feel the same energy flowing in the neighbour's house, in the whole society, in the whole city, town, state, country, world, in the cosmic beings like sun, moon, stars and other constellations, Milky Way.

Feel this energy flowing from every cell in your body and the moment you are able to understand and accept the fact that you are nothing but a small speck in the creations of the Lord and the energy flowing through you is no greater than the one flowing through others.

BENEFITS OF DOING THIS DHYANA

1. The nadis of the Heart chakra gets cleansed and balancing happens between the Heart chakra and the minor chakras related with it.
2. Continuous practice of this meditation helps in purification of thinking process thereby helping to balance the Ida nadi
3. The flow of emotions is higher during this dhyana and it helps in dissolving all the past karmic deeds for a better future.

Note:

- The Detailed explanations of the Chakras are provided in the Chakra Section.
- The advanced levels are covered in the author's book "Soul Searchers- The Hidden Mysteries of Kundalini"

Spiritual Meditation Series #3

SPIRITUAL HUMMING TECHNIQUE (SHT)

This technique works on the pattern of the music syllables. Both western and Indian musical syllables are provided and the channel can use any one of them for achieving success in the meditation.

Western Musical Syllable

Do - Re - Mi - Fa - So - La - Ti - Do

Indian Musical Syllable

Sa - Re - Ga - Ma - Pa - Dha - Ni - Sa

Sa/ Do will use a deep vocal sound in the beginning and this will go shallow and sharp by the time it reaches the Do/ Sa in the end. Each syllable represents the seven celestial chakras in our body. The explanations of the concept of Chakras are given in the Chakra Section.

This technique is found to be powerful enough to bring in drastic changes in the individual practitioner. If the practitioner has interest in singing or music then the energy stored in these powerful musical syllables gets transmitted throughout the environment causing cleansing of the negative thoughts and energies.

CHAKRA

Indian Name Name	Western	Sound	Location
Mooladhara	Base	Do / Sa	Two finger below the genital organ
Swadhisthana	Sacral	Re	Genital Organ
Manipura	Navel	Mi / Ga	Navel
Anahata	Heart	Fa / Ma	Two finger to the right of the heart
Vishuddhi	Throat	So / Pa	Throat
Aagya	Third eye	La / Dha	Centre of the eyebrows
Sahasrara	Crown	Ti / Ni	Top of the head
Syambhu	Spirit	Do / Sa	Two inches above the head

PROCESS OF DOING THIS MEDITATION

Note : Before you start this meditation memorise all the syllables and their related chakras.

STEP#1

Sit down comfortably on a chair with the hands on the lap. The palms should face the sky. Close your eyes and take three deep breaths. Inhale to a count of four and exhale to a count six or eight. Repeat this process for three times. During the process of inhalation feel your body covered with glowing white universal light and during exhalation feel that the universal light is taking away all the stresses and strains from your body.

STEP#2

Place your right palm over the Mooladhara chakra, and let the left hand be above your head (palm facing the sky).

Say **SA.. SA.. SA.. SA.. SA.. SA.. SA** the syllable should be said in the deepest of the voice. The voice should be raised from the lowest to the highest pitch.

STEP#3

Place your right palm over the Swadhisthana chakra, and let the left hand be above your head (palm facing the sky).

Say **RE.. RE.. RE.. RE.. RE.. RE.. RE** the syllable should be said in deep voice. The voice should be raised from the lowest to the highest pitch.

STEP#4

Place your right palm over the Manipura chakra, and let the left hand be above your head (palm facing the sky).

Say **GA..GA..GA..GA..GA..GA..GA** the syllable should be said in the Normal voice The voice should be raised from the Normal level to the highest pitch.

STEP#5

Place your right palm over the Anahata chakra, and let the left hand be above your head (palm facing the sky).

Say **MA..MA..MA..MA..MA..MA..MA** the syllable should be said in the Shallow level. The voice should be raised from the Shallow level to the highest pitch.

STEP #6

Place your right palm over the Vishuddhi chakra, and let the left hand be above your head (palm facing the sky).

Say **PA..PA..PA..PA..PA..PA..PA** the syllable should be said in the slightly higher level voice The voice should be raised from the slightly higher level to the highest pitch.

STEP#7

Place your right palm over the Ajna chakra, and let the left hand be above your head (palm facing the sky).

Say **DHA.. DHA.. DHA.. DHA.. DHA.. DHA.. DHA** the syllable should be said in the higher level of voice The voice should be raised from the higher level to the highest pitch.

STEP#8

Place your right palm over the Sahasrara chakra, and let the left hand be above your head (palm facing the sky).

Say **NI..NI..NI..NI..NI..NI..NI** the syllable should be said in the highest level of voice.

STEP#9

Place your right palm over the Syambhu chakra, and let the left hand be above your head (palm facing the sky).

Say **SA..SA..SA..SA..SA..SA..SA** the syllable should be said in the Highest pitch.

STEP # 10

Repeat the process of healing from the Step # 9 to Step # 2.

Note : Start by doing steps 1 to 9, only after gaining confidence should you proceed on with the whole process i.e. from Step 1 to 10.

Spiritual Meditation Series #4

SPIRITUAL HUMMING TECHNIQUE (SHT) FOR HOUSE PURIFICATION TECHNIQUE (HPT)

Music is said to be the most important and powerful methods of energisation of the nature's creation. We have already given the **Spiritual Humming Technique**, which can be used for the betterment of the self-energy and also for the energising the room in which you are meditating.

The purpose of this technique is to compel you to experiment with the energy that is all around you and also to tap the sources of the energy so that the expenditure of the energy is optimally utilized or spent.

- This technique will enhance the positive energy in the room and will dispel the negative energy from being accumulated in the room.
- Before the start of meditation sit facing the north direction.
- If you have a Wind Chime/ Mirror/ Painting/ Ba Gua diagram in front of you send the voice energies to those Feng Shui energy images.
- If none of the above are available then send the Sound energy to all the sides of the room.
- Regular sending of the energy to the Feng Shui energy symbols will enhance the flow of the positive energy to the room.

BENEFITS OF THIS EXERCISE

1. Balancing of energy centres of the body.
2. Activation of the Major chakras and also energisation of the chakras.
3. If combined with Feng Shui technique then the energy will flow immensely throughout the house.

Spiritual Meditation Series #5

KI PARTNER

Ki partner is a unique technique, which works wonders for developmental activities. Ki partner is a spiritual energy, which works like a guide and keeps you in contact with the universal energy. This is a useful technique for those people who have regular meeting for signing contracts, developing business plans, studies etc. Many people have benefited from this technique.

MATERIALS REQUIRED FOR THIS TECHNIQUE

1. A square white paper (minimum measuring 2" by 2")
2. Pen with Red/ Orange ink, Sketch pens can also be used.
3. A hard base on which the paper can be kept.

STEPS FOR DOING THIS TECHNIQUE

- Sit in a comfortable position. Place the hard base in front of you with the paper on top of it. Say a Prayer to the universal energy for blessing you with energy for the creation of the Ki partner
- Sit in the comfortable position till you feel the energy of the universe flowing through your fingertips.
- Take the pen in your right hand and give the energy to the pen with your left hand. While giving the energy to the pen feel the universal white light entering your Crown Chakra and flowing down through the Throat chakra, Heart chakra and to flow out from the finger tips.
- Now keep the pen on the centre of the paper and place both your hands on the paper in such a way that you cover the paper as well as the pen. Give energy to the paper as well as the pen for five minutes.

- Draw a human figure on the centre of the paper. Remember that what you draw is going to be your partner for the achievement of your goals.
- Place both your hands on the drawing (the whole of the drawing should be covered). Let the energy pass through your hands to the picture you have drawn.
- Now chant the following

I am thankful to the Universal Energy for helping me
I am thankful to all the Masters
I now announce that Ki is my partner
He will there to guide me for immediate purpose
(Disclose the purpose of creating Ki)
I thank all for helping me, for blessing me
Thank you, thank you

- Now your Ki partner is ready to help you in your project. Place the photograph in the left shirt pocket while going for the project/ purpose.
- Just before starting the process say the following lines

I am thankful for Universal Energy being here
I am thankful Ki partner being here

• Ki partner is now ready for helping you. Ki partner will guide you mentally and spiritually for the achievement of your goals.

HOW TO DISSOLVE THE KI PARTNER

After achievement of the purpose, burn the Ki partner. After burning the paper, scatter the pieces in a flowerpot or submerge it in a river.

Note: Never tear, flush or throwaway the Ki partner paper

Spiritual Meditation Series #6

CONCENTRATION- DE-CONCENTRATION #1

Many times you must have felt that whatever work you do you are not in a position to concentrate on the job. There can be many reasons for this like lack of concentration, stress, tension, lack of motivation etc. All these can individually or in combination affect the working of the individual and this leads to the occurrence of the problems in home and office. In the later stage this can develop in to a psychosomatic problem for which the solution will not be easy.

This technique will provide the correct methodology of doing a work and also provide the energy to encompass the future results in advance and then work towards achieving the goal.

STEP#1

This technique can be done at any period of time including the office.

This meditation involves the process of understanding the movement of body.

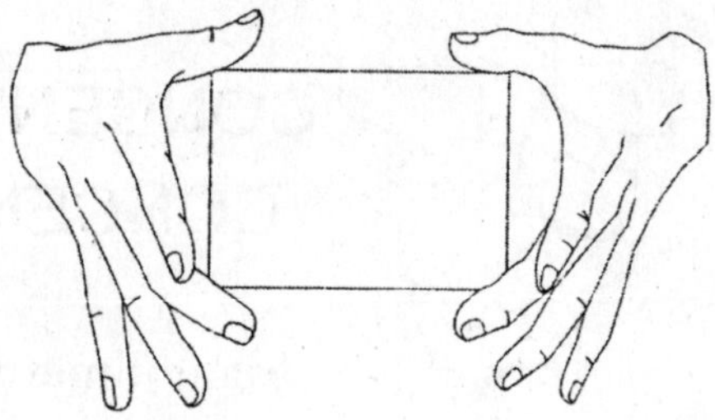

Inhale and Exhale deeply for ten times and release all the tensions from the mind.

Move your right hand over the heart region and observe the movement of the muscles in the arm for the action. Every single movement has to be observed in a conscious manner.

Extend this observation to various other body movements like walking, pulling or pushing things, scratching etc.

This exercise can be extended to movement of eyes, mouth, nose, neck muscles etc.

STEP#2

Inhale and Exhale deeply for ten times and release all the tensions from the mind.

Keep breathing in a normal manner and continue the process as described above. The difference is to understand the movements of the body parts rather than just observing them. For example while moving your hand feel the movement and tension of muscles.

This technique would provide a relaxation of the muscle tissues and also provide a soothing experience to the eyes.

STEP#3

Inhale and Exhale deeply for ten times and release all the tensions from the mind.

Keep breathing in a normal manner and continue the process as described above in step #1.

The difference here is to feel the effect of the movement on other parts of the body. For example while moving your hand feel the change of position of the shoulder, chest and stomach region.

This technique helps in expanding the area of concentration.

Regular practice of the above three steps would help in

- Understanding the body in a better manner
- Development of the better concentration
- Students if they practice this technique during the examination period would help them to concentrate better.

Spiritual Meditation Series #7

PART OF THE UNIVERSE

The cycle of birth and death is a continuous process which has been stressed by thousands of saints for ages together and it is only when a person gets to know his own true self, he finds the real purpose of his existence. How can an individual get to know his real self without first knowing himself first. This is a peculiar problem that has been haunting a layman for ages. He was given to understand that by knowing oneself would automatically know the true self but never provided with a technique for reaching deep inside to find the truth himself. Even those who have delved deep inside were reluctant to provide this technique for the benefit of the masses.

This is a unique technique that helps an individual to help and understand the existence of the cosmos inside our physical body. This technique uses the visualisation skills of the practitioner and allows them to develop to such an extent that it encompasses the whole physical self itself. Regular practice of this technique can provide a sense of belonging, a sense of being a part of the vast universe.

This technique can be done any time of the day, but the preferred time would be early morning.

STEP#1

BEGINNING

(Five minutes)

Sit or lie down comfortably. Place the right hand over the centre of the chest and close your eyes. Breathe slowly and continuously and feel the heart beats against the palm. Synchronise the breathing with the heartbeat. On every beat inhale and on every gap exhale.

At the end of five minutes move the right-hand near the right side of the body, but continue to breathe in the similar manner so that the rhythm is maintained. The awareness of the heartbeat should also be maintained.

STEP#2

AWARENESS

(Five minutes)

The awareness of the heartbeat should be full and final. The meaning of this is that when awareness is at the heart centre, rest of the body should cease to exist.

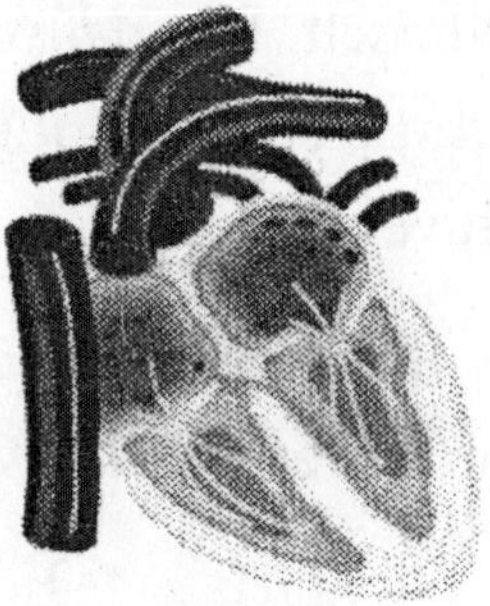

You can also visualise the heart pumping the blood to various part of the body. The clearer the visualisation the better would be the awareness.

Continue to be in the state of total uninterrupted state of heart awareness.

STEP#3

DEVELOPING THE AWARENESS

(Five minutes)

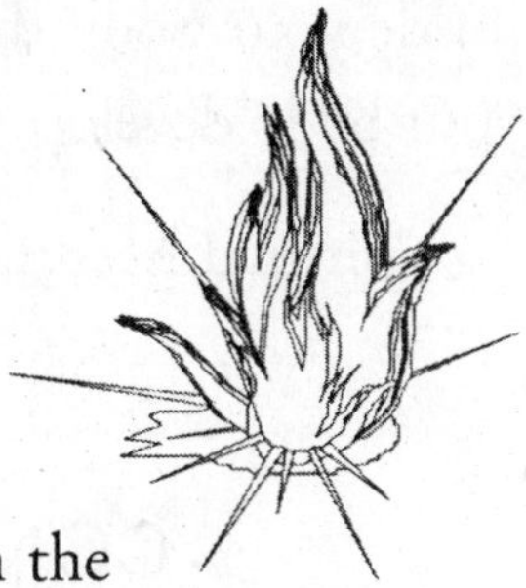

In this stage visualise a beautiful blue flame emitting from the heart area. This blue flame has three shades; the innermost part of the flame is having pure yellow flame and second part with red flame. The flames of this divine fire are the total essence of the heart energy.

Feel with each breath that the flames are getting the energy to spread out to the entire vicinity and providing the peaceful and harmonious energy to the total being. This energy will provide peace and a sense of happiness to your body and help to get your body rejuvenated with energy.

The above steps will take you from the basic or gross levels of thinking to a level of awareness of energy situated

> I have only devices and answers; the answer itself is dependent upon you. The way you perceive so do, I come out with an answer unique to you. So it is you who provide me with the question as well as answer.

inside your body that is actually the power of making your body develop and move as per the requirement.

Spiritual Meditation Series #8

CONCENTRATION-DE-CONCENTRATION # 2

Human beings are blessed with the thinking power and the thoughts are like a flowing river, which has tremendous untapped potential. The thoughts that can either create or destroy the whole existence of the human being.

From the ancient times control of thoughts were the main aim of many sadhakas. Most of the scriptures prescribe that the thoughts to be controlled for achieving the Dhyana required for reaching the Supreme Being, but never prescribed the method for controlling the thoughts.

The following techniques though different in nature provide the control over the thoughts within a short period of time. These techniques can be done at any period of time and can also be done easily in office also.

Note: Do not do this technique in office when you are doing some work which requires concentration or attention.

LET THE THOUGHTS FLOW....

As mentioned above the thoughts are like flowing river sometime slow and sometime very fast and the thoughts come in abundance and distract your attention and thus creating mistakes in the work.

In the beginning while doing this technique, it is quite possible that a sense of disturbance may creep in but as you go on practicing this technique the level of disturbance will come down and at one stage your mind will become calm and quiet.

The technique is to allow the thoughts to flow. Let

it flow through your mind, body and soul freely without any hindrance. No restriction whatsoever should be placed on the thoughts, nor should be attached with the thoughts. The thoughts should be like a movie that is running in front of you and you should be in no way affected by it.

This technique should be followed only after getting well versed in the above technique. The danger of working on this technique before getting mastery of the above technique is that there is chance of getting blank thoughts passing through the mind at frequent rate.

Whenever it is possible, try to observe your thoughts during the day. Evaluate the way you are thinking and feeling. Learn to understand yourself and your thought patterns.

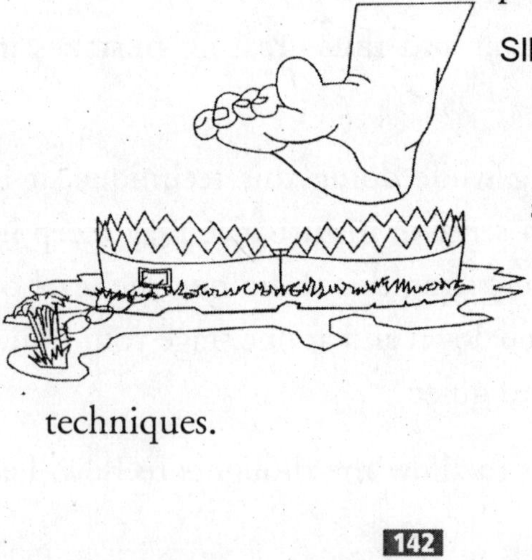

SILENCED THOUGHTS

This technique should be followed after getting experience in the above two techniques.

In this technique try and control the thought process so that the individual experience and other egos should melt away leading to the emergence of the pure thoughtless situation.

Stay in this thoughtless state as long as you want and this thoughtless state has been called the state of samadhi, mouna dhyana or a state of nirvana.

ADVANCED SILENCED THOUGHTS

The above technique becomes more powerful when you are able to sleep while doing this technique. The sleep will be more of a Yogic-sleep, where the body has no role to play while it is totally encompassing the role of the soul and the Supreme Being.

You are not required to have any concentration, but being in the state of thoughtlessness, which is the most beautiful experience that any practitioner would like to be in.

Regular practice of these techniques can help to provide the state of thoughtless stature within a short span of time.

> A master doesnot have anything but he gains happiness by helping others, he gets richer by distributing his knowledge.

3 levels of Awareness

FIRST AWARENESS

Watch your actions, reactions and the responses to it. Watching your own actions, reactions and responses will bring you the awareness about what exactly you are a MAN or a MACHINE. Machines are mechanical and function in the similar manner and humans in 99 out of 100 situations unction in a mechanical manner. He has certain past conditions that form the basis for the current judgment.

The second awareness happens when you are bit more alert then the concept of current happening becomes a part of you. Though you are stimulated by the past conditions yet the decision is based upon the current situation. This awareness is the first step out of the mechanical process of decision-making and a new awareness of the MAN takes place inside.

Third awareness is the stage when you are fully in the present and take decision based upon the current situation. Every similar situation will bring out a new decision and then the similarity would cease to exist a new creation will happen. Full awareness of man will happen only when there is complete annihilation of the mechanical process.

Spiritual Meditation Series #9

THE VOID

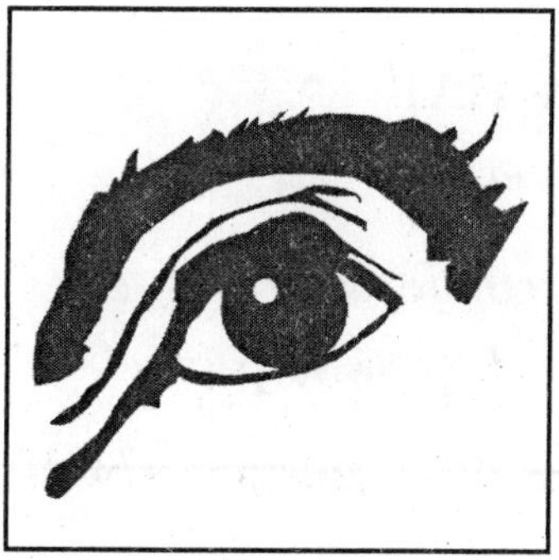

Thoughts are the most beautiful thing that human beings are blessed with. No individual can live without thoughts. They are part and parcel of the human mind. It is created and emitted from the conscious and sub-conscious mind.

Thoughts are mostly dependent on moods as in happy times we enjoy only the happy thoughts while in a depressed the same thoughts get transformed into sad and disheartening thoughts.

If we are able to block the thoughts for a particular period of time we will be able to see and feel the supra-conscious mind. This is the powerhouse that resides in the most remote corner of the mind. Tapping this source of energy would unleash the true potential of the human mind.

The following technique would provide a simple yet effective method of achieving this powerful feeling. This is a dynamic method of meditation so it is advisable that it should not be done during emotional upheavals.

STEP # 1

WATCHING WHAT

(Time- 20 minutes)

For doing this technique sit comfortably with erect spine facing a blank wall or a white piece of paper.

The technique is to observe the blank paper/wall very minutely.

Continue watching the paper till you feel a sense of blankness coming over you.

It is possible you may feel some sense of fear or vibrations in the upper spinal column. Donot leave the meditation continue with the process.

STEP#2

WATCHING SKY

(Time - 20 minutes)

This meditation is best done in outdoors when the sky is clear or has little clouds. **Never do this method when the sun is high or in the night with full of stars.**

For doing this technique lie down comfortably; feet apart and hands on the side. The technique is to observe the clear sky minutely.

Continue watching the sky till you feel a sense of blankness/ sleepiness coming over you. Donot close your eyes; otherwise you will fall asleep and that we donot want.

Continuous practice of this meditation would bring in the awareness that the physical body is just another extension of the inner body.

❋❋❋

Energy moving meditations

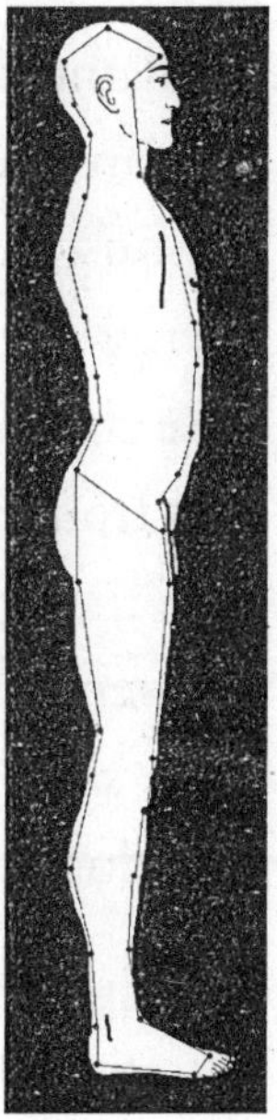

Have you ever seen ants going in a row. It is really a fantastic view, they move in such a harmonious manner that from a distance it looks as if a black thick line is drawn on the wall. Human body is also synchronised by the universal energy and only those who have understood the energy within can really climb on the ladder of success.

For understanding the strengths of the inner body it is important to understand the basics of the flow of energy inside of our body.

Human body is a unique cosmic machinery working continuously for ages together on the basis of the eternal wheels of energy. The moment we are able to tap these energy centres we get a new leash of life. These energy wheels are called chakras.

Chakras start their work when a person is in the womb itself but externally a person never comes in contact with them unless and until he works towards reaching them.

Kundalini is the universal power that resides in the human body in the dormant state and until awakened a person cannot achieve much in the spiritual field. This energy is represented as a snake in 3 1/2 coils at the Base chakra. When this center is activated, the Kundalini rises from the Base chakra and reaches the Crown chakra; this rising has been termed as enlightenment. The moment a practitioner is able to activate the Kundalini he is said to become a complete Yogi, one who is in non-dual state of divine union and bliss.

I had covered more than 547 chakras in *"Soul Searchers- The Hidden Mysteries of Kundalini"*, but since such huge details are not required in this book, I will be explaining about them in very brief.

For this book, I will be covering the basic information regarding the Seven Major chakras in the body. These are said to be located in the inner side of the spinal column, not visible to naked eyes or any man made machines. These are powerhouses that control each and every movement of man from the stage of inception to the stage of death.

Each of these chakras is represented in the shape of a lotus flower and every chakra has its own unique function and processes.

MOOLADHARA/BASE CHAKRA

Mooladhara chakra is the most important chakra of the body located two fingers below the testis and two fingers above the anus. Mooladhara derives the name from **Moola** meaning **root** and **adhara** meaning **Base**, this chakra forms the base of the

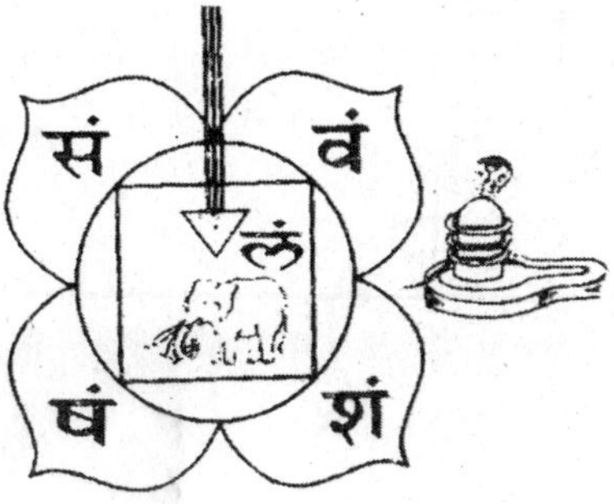

spine and also the other chakras of the body. This chakra is red in colour.

SWADHISTHANA CHAKRA

Swadhisthana chakra means **Swa** and **Adhisthana** meaning under ones own control. Swadishtana chakra is situated two fingers above the Mooladhara chakra and is vermilion red in colour. This chakra is responsible for all the urinary, excretory, reproduction system and water related needs of the body. Physically the chakra is located on the base of the spinal column with the pubic bone.

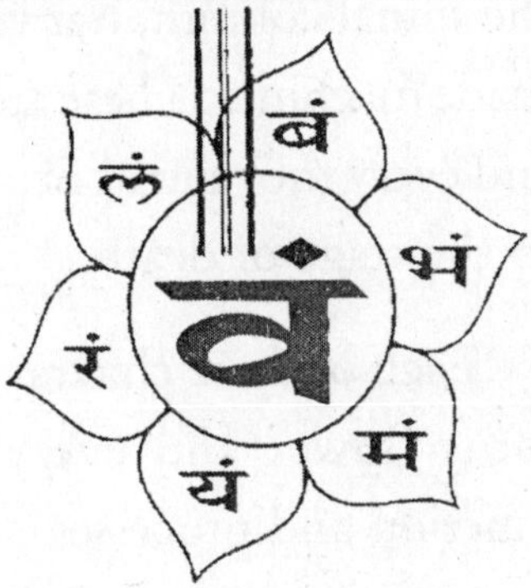

MANIPURA/NAVEL CHAKRA

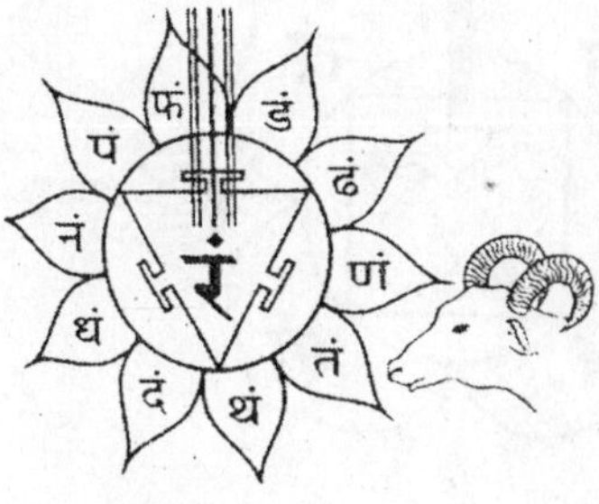

This chakra is also called as the Navel chakra as the position of this chakra resides in the navel. The name of this chakra is derived from two words 'Mani' and 'Pura' meaning Jewel and Place, thereby meaning the place where jewels are found. The Tibetan mantra Om Mani Padme Hum is for this chakra where Mani Padme means 'jewelled lotus'. Navel chakra is dark greyish in colour.

ANAHATA/HEART CENTRE

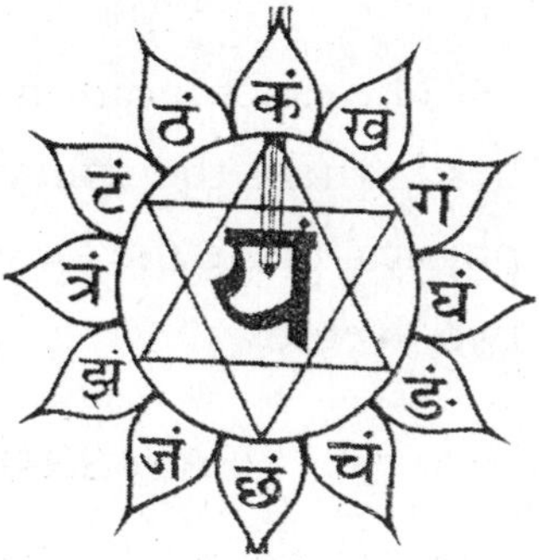

Anahata means endless love and pacification. The physical part of the body where the chakra is located is heart. This chakra is responsible for the correct working of the lungs and the heart. This chakra is deep red in colour.

VISHUDDHI/THROAT CENTRE

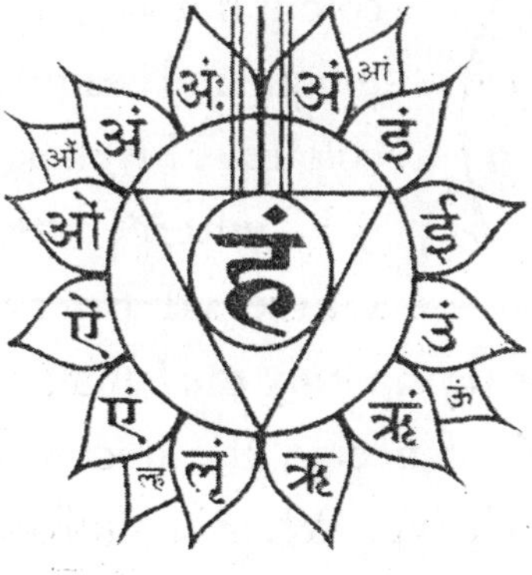

Vishuddhi chakra is located in the throat where the collarbones meet. This chakra is responsible for the correct functioning of the throat, vocal cord, upper lungs, mouth and nose. This is Deep blue in colour.

AJNA/THIRD EYE CHAKRA

The exact location of the Ajna chakra is behind the head where the spinal cord meets the brain. On the physical plane the location of the chakra is between the two eyebrows.

SAHASRARA/CROWN CHAKRA

Sahasrara is actually not a chakra but the energy of the universe itself. Sahasrara means thousand petalled lotuses. This chakra does not have one colour but has many unique and beautiful colours. This chakra is where the Universal Energy meets the Creator. Due to this reason only the Sahasrara chakra is called the fountain of nectar, the nectar of spiritual and universal knowledge. When a sadhaka

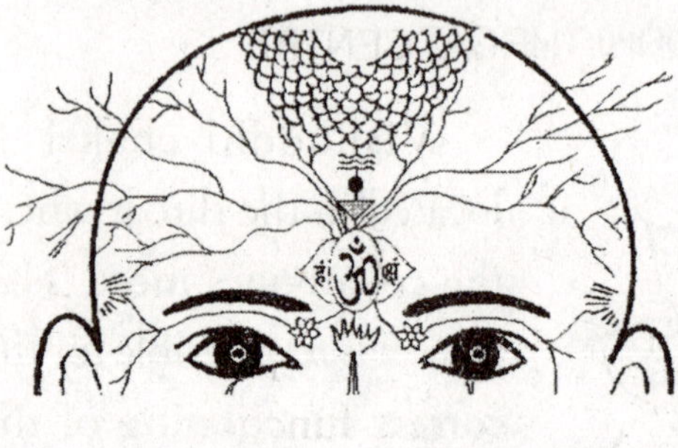

reaches this stage he achieves the knowledge of the past present and the future.

The information provided about the chakra is just a simple and rough outline, but it will serve our purpose of working towards the goal.

Meditation in this section are more developed as compared to other two sections you have covered as from this section onwards the concentration will be on the development of the prana / Chi energy for the achievement of our various goals. This section if practiced for longer period of time can awaken the chakra, for the meditation effects. I have personally seen the Kundalini rising by practicing of these techniques, but that requires very long period of time.

Thus, it is important for the benefit of the practitioners that they cover the first two sections of the book for better understanding of the flow of energy as also the various techniques that will help an individual to become adaptable to the following techniques.

No river remains the same ever, every wave changes the riverforever.

Energy Moving Meditation Series #1

ENERGY SPOT ECHNIQUE (EST)

For any healer the important thing is to get energised with the universal energy, this energy will in turn help the healer to achieve inner strength to solve any kind of healing problems. EST is best done in the early morning on an empty stomach, or you should have a gap of three hours between the meals.

Process of doing this technique

- Stand on a mat with hands in front of you and the palms facing the sky. Back should be kept erect and the feet should be little parted.
- Concentrate fully on the Base Chakra (Mooladhara Chakra). The location being the genital area.

- Stand still till you feel sensation in your hands and fingertips.

STAGE # 1

- Place your left hand over the Mooladhara chakra and raise the right hand above you. Right hand will work as antennae and the left hand will work as the responder.

- Say the following in your mind

O Lord help me with the universal energy
Balance the Base chakra
with all the Nerves connected to it

Move the left hand over to the Swadhisthana chakra, keeping the right hand above the head. Say the following in your mind

O Lord help me with the universal energy
Balance the Swadhisthana chakra
and all the minor chakras and
the Nerves connected to it

- Move the left hand over to the Manipura (Navel) chakra and the right hand over the heart chakra. Say the following in your mind

O Lord help me with the universal energy
Balance the Navel chakra
and all the minor chakras and
the Nerves connected to it with the
Heart chakra.

- Move the left hand over to the Heart (Anahata) chakra keeping the right hand over the heart chakra. Say the following in your mind

O Lord help me with the universal energy
Balance the Heart chakra
with all the emotions and love
Like Mother Nature Fill me with
Love for everyone.

- Move the left hand over to the Vishuddhi (Throat) chakra keeping the right hand over the heart chakra. Say the following in your mind

O Lord help me with the universal energy
Balance the Vishuddhi chakra
with the heart chakra and all the minor chakras
associated with it.

Move the left hand over to the Aagya (Third eye) chakra keeping the right hand over the heart chakra. Say the following in your mind

O Lord help me with the universal energy
Balance the Aagya chakra
With the heart chakra and all the minor chakras
Associated with it.
Let the beholder of this energy be blessed
With the energy of the universe

STAGE # 2

- Repeat the Stage #1 using the right hand as responder and left hand as the antennae

Note :

- In all the above stages, keep the hands on a particular chakra for a period of three minutes.
- If the practitioner is doing this technique lying down then place a pillow under the feet.
- There should be a gap of atleast 4 hours between the meal and meditation

In a departmental store, a man approached a beautiful woman in a state of distress. He went on his knees and said "Please talk to me, I need your help?" Woman feeling embarrassed asked the man to stand up and asked for the reason. The man replied, "My wife had taken my purse and at the counter the cashier wants the payment. My wife is nowhere to be seen. If you talk to me she will appear instantaneously." He hadn't finished saying this the wife appeared out of now where.

Life is like a wife ignore it and it will confront you.

Energy Moving Meditation Series #2

NATURAL MEDITATION

This is a unique meditational technique I learnt from the God's own creation, a child. This is the most active meditational process that heightens your internal capabilities to reach further into the spiritual path of progress.

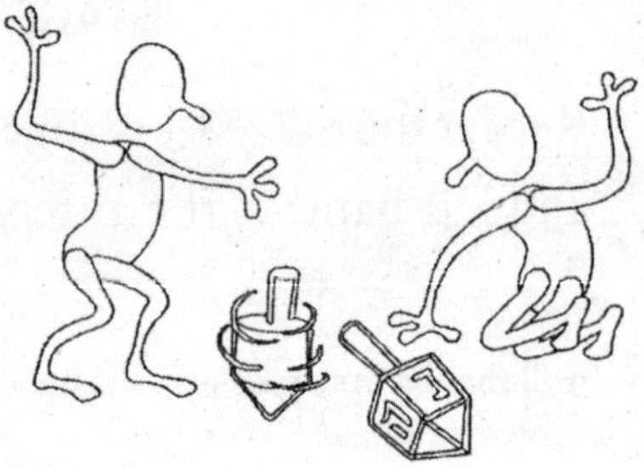

Note: It is important that this meditation is done only after getting permission from medical expert if the practitioner is suffering from any of the medical problems.

Before you do this meditation process the following things are to be kept in mind:

- The dress should be loose and comfortable as this meditation required lots of body movements.
- The place where this meditation is done should have lot of free space.

- Have a big rug placed in the room where the meditation is to be done.
- This type of dhyana is more fruitful if done in absolute silence, as this exercise will allow you to see the true person in you.

PROCESS#1

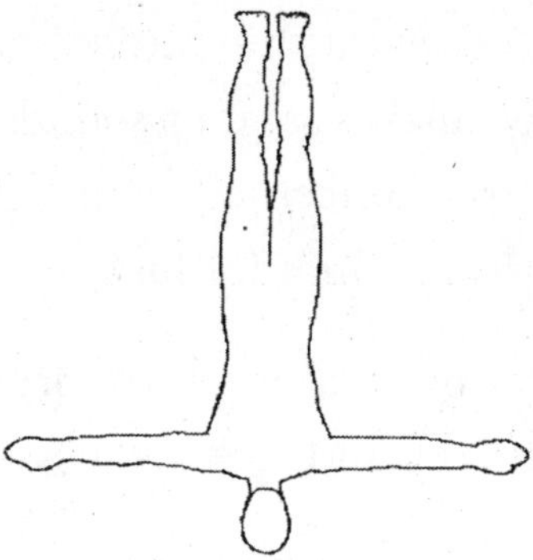

Lie down on the rug with the hands placed on the sides as shown in the diagram.

Close your eyes and breath in a normal manner for a few minutes till you get the flow of your breath inside your body.

Breathe from the stomach, with each inhalation the expansion of stomach occurs first, then the chest expands and lastly the thorax region expands-similarly on exhalation the thorax region subsides then the chest and lastly the stomach subsides.

Continue doing this kind of breathing for five minutes.

PROCESS # 2

Have you ever observed a child playing by himself in the pram? The child is totally absorbed within himself he talks to himself, sucks his own toe, makes gargling sounds, does speed cycling etc. He is not concerned with the people around nor the sounds distract him for long.

Similarly in this meditation, we will work towards achieving the similar kind of energy and attentiveness.

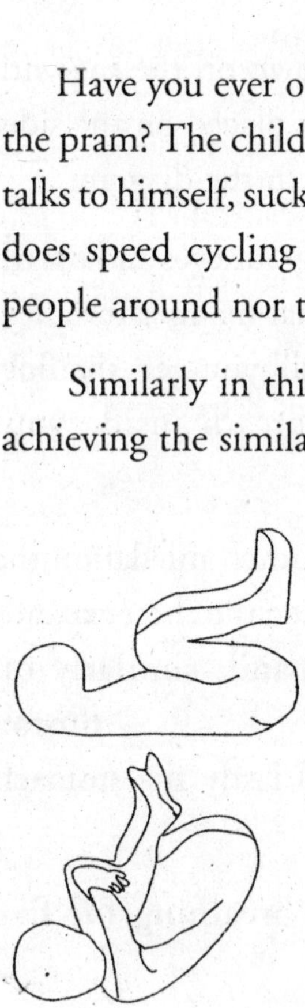

Lying in the same posture as shown in the first step, raise the knees towards the chest slowly. When you feel that you have reached the maximum level, stop and feel the strain at the lower back, stomach, shoulders, calf-muscles, thighs and groin region.

Keeping the strain on the above body parts, turn your body to left and hold for a slow count of 10.

Come back to the normal position as in the beginning and then turn your body towards the right and hold for a slow count of 10.

Return to the normal position release the thighs and lie in the position shown in step 1. Continue to be in this position for a period of five minutes.

PROCESS#3

Slowly bring both the palms on the navel and keep breathing normally. Feel the upward and downward movement of the stomach.

Slowly count to 10 and inhale deeply. Close your right palm into a fist and raise your right palm towards the air. When you raise the hand, feel all the power from the body is moving with the hand. Hold for a count of two and bring back the right hand to the navel.

Repeat the process using the left hand.

Continue this process for a period of ten rounds, and then repeat the Step 1.

PROCESS # 4

Tense all the muscles in the feet for two rounds of breathing (Inhale-Exhale, Inhale-Exhale) and release the tension.

Repeat the above process with calf muscles, thigh, hip, lower abdomen, abdomen, chest, shoulder, hands, neck, face, one by one.

Repeat the Step 1 again.

In this meditational process, I have covered three different techniques for providing you with the supply of energy for the whole day. You can either select one of the techniques or do all the three, but donot ignore to release yourself with the Step 1 after each technique.

Energy Moving Meditation Series #2

NATURAL SENSATION

Nature has a galore of surprise for us ı store it is only that we have to just ıxtend our hands to get those beautiful things in our possession.

This technique is unique in nature, as it will provide the practitioner with the power of cooling himself within a short period of time.

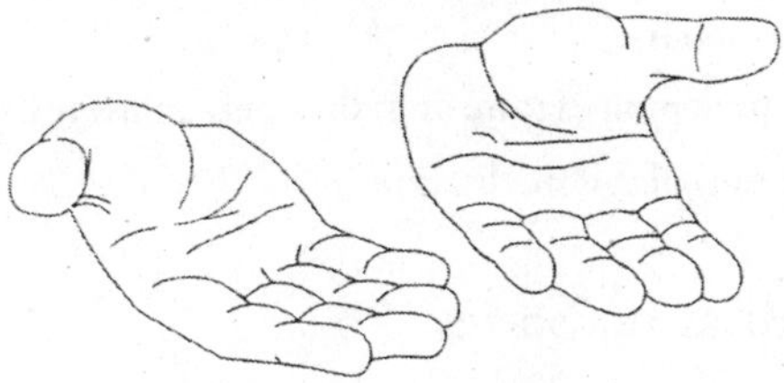

Sit comfortably on a chair and place the hands on the knees, the palms of hands facing the sky. The palms should be in a cup shape, so that you are able to hold the energy flow.

Observe both your palms closely. Then close your eyes and concentrate on the tips of the fingers.

Breathe normally during the whole process, after some time you will feel a sensation in your hands. It will start from the fingertips and flow to the centre of the palm.

The more the sensation spreads the more cooler your body becomes. Sit in posture for some time and if you are able to visualise your whole body then you will feel the sensation moving throughout your entire body.

It is marvelous that people have had this power within themselves but were ignorant about it. The sensation happens because hands are very sensitive due to which it has the ability to feel and understand. The reason for this sensitive nature is due to the fact that the extremities of the blood circulation system are located here.

Note:

- This meditation is best done indoors.
- Never do this meditation in peak temperature or in the open unless you become adept in the finer aspects of this meditation.

Energy Moving Meditation Series #3

ALTERNATIVE TECHNIQUE TO NATURAL BREATHING

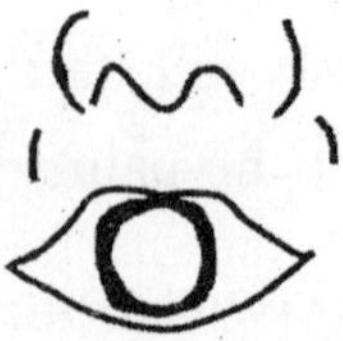

Sit comfortably on a chair and place the hands on the knees. The position of the hands is not important.

Inhale deeply and exhale deeply for ten times.

Part the lips slightly and let the tongue come out of the mouth. Bend the two sides of the tongue towards the centre forming a 'U' shape.

Inhale from the curved tongue slowly and when you feel you have reached a maximum level stop and after taking the tongue in the mouth, close the mouth tightly.

You will feel a surge of cold waves filling your lungs completely. This method is called Sheetli Kriya in Yoga and is used to cool body temperature.

You can repeat this method, as many times as possible and every time the body temperature will come down.

Benefits of Meditation

- This technique is a marvellous technique that can be done at peak temperature. It works in the outdoors also.

Energy Moving Meditation Series #4

POWER ENERGISATION

This is powerful exercise for focusing the energy at the desired place. Regular practice of this technique will help in using the life force energies in a better manner and also restrict the wastage of the energy in any manner.

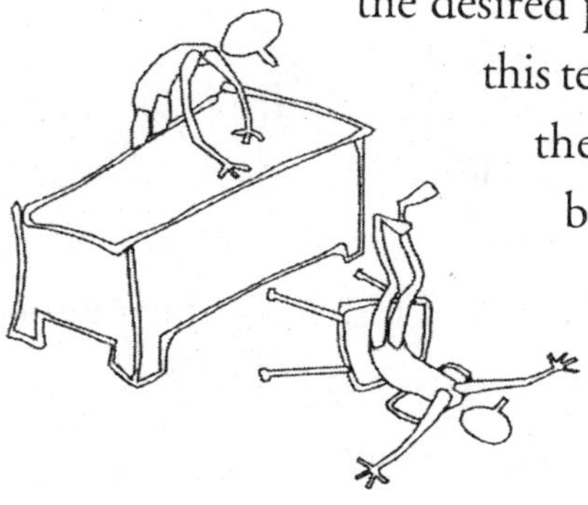

Note : This is a powerful method and thus it is important that you respect the technique and work as given in the instructions, donot mix any other techniques of yours with this technique.

As this technique works on the thin line of energy and physical body it is quite possible for opening the third eye with this technique.

STEP#1

Start with the *Moving Meditation #1- Standing Alone.*

Breathe in slowly and release slowly, repeat this process for five times.

Part the legs to the shoulder width. Place both the hands on the hip and close your eyes.

Tighten your leg muscles starting from the toes, ankles, calf, thighs, groin and hip. Hold the tension for a period of thirty seconds and release it.

Keeping the eyes closed feel that powerful forces are pulling you from all the directions. Feel the head being pulled up towards the sky by an unknown powerful force, similarly feel that the feet being drawn below the ground by an unknown powerful force and both the hands are being pulled in both the directions.

During the whole process, continue breathing deeply but slowly. When you feel really tense then release the tension by swinging hands up and down and doing two three slow jogging steps.

But never ever loose the concentration on the energy pulling on your body and donot open your eyes. Do this technique for two rounds.

Some points

- Do this exercise in the morning only.
- Repeat the process of meditation for a period of fifteen days atleast to gain the benefits.
- Once you start feeling that a bursting force developing in the stomach, start the second step.

STEP#2

Keep breathing as in Step #1, concentrate on the Base Chakra and start breathing into the said chakra.

While sending the breath energy to the Base chakra, the eyeballs should be centered on the centre of the eyebrows. Continue doing this till you feel the force in the stomach has subsided.

Step #3, 4, 5, 6

Repeat the Step 2 with the Swadhisthana chakra.

Repeat the Step 2 with the Navel Chakra.

Repeat the Step 2 with the Heart chakra.

Repeat the Step 2 with the Throat chakra.

These steps should only be done if the feeling of the energy returns after a lapse of certain period.

After a period of two months of practice, you will be amazed to see the increase in the focus levels. And if you continue to do the meditations for ten minutes daily, then you will get the power of activating the energy whenever you want.

Energy Moving Meditation Series #5

ENERGY SHIELD

For every successful person,
There will be ten enemies,
For every saint there will be ten devils
For every God there will be ten Satan's.

This old saying aptly works in all fields of life. Spiritual seekers in their quest for acquiring the universal energy activated the energies, which were feared by the common people. The fear arises because they cannot comprehend this unique energy and they started hating such people. In their hatredness, they knowingly or unknowingly sent out negative energies, which hampered the progress of the spiritual seekers. The spiritual seekers also started hating people who were ahead of them in acquiring the universal energy and due to this they caused worst damage.

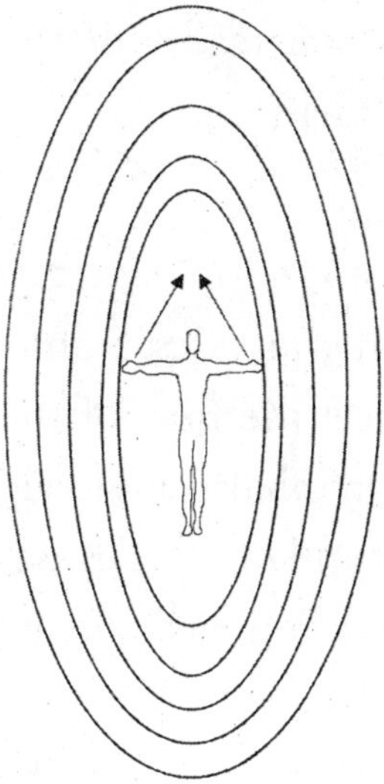

I am providing here a simple but effective protective energy shield that can be used by anybody for protection against evil forces, which can cause damage.

Start with the *Moving Meditation #1- Standing Alone.*

Breathe in slowly and release slowly, repeat this process for five times.

Part the legs to the shoulder width. Place both the hands on the hip and close your eyes.

Pull your anus up to by contracting the anus and lower abdominal muscles.

Power of Prana Technique:

Inhale deeply and exhale deeply for five times. Hold the breath for a count of ten. Now you ready for the Power of Prana Technique/ Energy Shield.

STEP#1

Slowly bring both the hands on the sides, palms facing upwards. Inhale deeply and feel the flow of the breathe being directed to the palms. On inhalation slowly raise both the hands towards the head and on exhalation, turn the palm facing the floor and come back to the original position.

Repeat this process ten times.

STEP#2

In this process, the hands would be raised to the shoulder sides keeping the palms upwards. The breathing would be similar to the Step #1, except in this case during exhalation the energy so retained would be sent out through the mouth in the form of visual cloud of energy.

Continue doing this energy blowing process till you feel that you are totally engulfed in the cloud of energy.

Mentally pray that this energy cloud should protect you from all the negative energies that can cause you harm. This is your personal energy shield.

This energy shield is so flexible that you can make uses of it. I have covered some of them in the following pages for the benefit of the readers.

Energy Moving Meditation Series #6

SELECTIVE ENERGY SHIELD
(uses for the energy shield)

It is possible to create an energy shield on a particular part of the body, which is useful while doing any sort of healing, psychic surgery etc.

While doing the step #2 concentrate, the flow of the

energy to the particular part of the body where you requires the shielding. After some time you will feel a sensation in that part and the shield is ready.

Healers can benefit from this technique, as it will provide them option for working out the energy shield in the manner they want.

Energy Moving Meditation Series #6

CHOCK- A-BLOCK (uses for the energy shield)

The biggest barrier in meditation or any work requiring focus of mind is the thought flow. Sometimes it so happens as soon as we sit for a work that requires a dedicated flow of energy in a particular direction the mind wavers and thoughts flow to all directions.

This technique would help you to block the unnecessary thoughts.

Do the step #2 technique with full concentration on the mind, particularly the hind part of the brain that works up thoughts and dreams.

After doing step#2, place the right hand behind the head and the left hand over the heart centre and mentally pray:

O Universal Lord,
The power of yours flows through me,
Shield, created with your energy
Covers the fragile body of mine
I pray to thee,
Withhold all the thoughts
Those that are unnecessary for me now
Let the doors of mind open to thoughts,
That will help me, guide me
And endow me with the knowledge
Of fulfilling the job undertaken
Let the shield be there to
Protect till <define the job>
Is complete as per desire of thee.

After the prayer resume the work and you will achieve total success within a short period of time.

This technique is also useful for people suffering from insomnia, depression, nervousness, tension etc.

Students can use this technique for developing laser sharp concentration.

Energy Moving Meditation Series #7

BALANCING THE FLOW OF ENERGY

It is seen that a person accumulates huge amount of diseases and other psychosomatic problems in the dormant state. These problems only manifest itself in the old age as by then the body loses out the strength and immunity.

This is a powerful technique that will help you energise every cell of yours to function as per the requirement and also provides strength and vitality to the inner immunity system.

Body Dear Body

STEP#1

For doing this technique, stand with feet shoulder width apart on a rug or a mat. Place the hands on the sides with the palms facing the floor.

Inhale deeply and exhale slowly for ten fifteen times. During the whole process of breathing, bring your awareness to the heart. On the physical level with each breath inhaled or exhaled feel the heart beat and on the psychic level feel the flow of the inhaled breathe inside your body.

It may be difficult in the beginning to concentrate on both the heartbeat as well as the flow of energy inside the body. But as you continue you will find to your surprise that the heart beat itself will lead you to the path of the energy flow.

STEP#2

Tense all the hand muscles keeping the palms facing towards the earth. Inhale deeply hold the breath and bring the hands towards the level of the chest.

When the hands are raised, the palms should move from facing the earth direction to face the front of the chest.

Release the breath with full force. The stress on releasing the breath should be felt at the navel and upper abdominal areas.

Relax all the muscles with the outflow of the breath.

Repeat the process for five times, then sit down quietly on the rug, close your eyes.

Concentration on the heart centre should not be released during the whole process.

Energy Moving Meditation Series #7

BALANCING THE FLOW OF ENERGY #2

The technique is similar to the Balancing of the Flow of Energy; the only difference is that in this case we will specify the flow of energy to a particular part of the body.

Repeat the Step #1 and Step #2 mentioned in the Balancing the Flow of Energy. The power of the energy released through the meditational technique as given above will form the basis for this technique.

In this technique let the energy flow through the problematic area. Let the tongue touch the upper palette, and the eye balls should be concentrating on the third eye or Aagya Chakra.

Move the palms to the area that is requiring the flow of energy. Place the palms over the area. If you are tensed or are in trouble then place the palms over the head.

Keeping the eyes concentrated at the third eye chakra feel the particular body part that requires healing or energisation. Inhale and draw in the stomach and let all the energy flow released by tucking in of the stomach to the concerned part of the body. Breathe deeply and exhale deeply several times until you feel calm and centered.

If you want you can also pray to increase the intensity of the flow of energy.

O Lord, Have mercy on this child of yours
Let the Energy that is being released
Become one from yours
Let thy divine energy, love and light
Heal all the problems that have weakened
The condition I am currently in
(Say the Concerned Problem)
Let I become pure and divine as you
Wanted me to become
Thank you thank you

This completes the technique. You may also do this technique for healing others.

Some important things to be known

- This technique should only be used for healing others once you have started understanding the flow of your own energy.
- Never waste this energy as it is the power that is residing in you, if excess energy is discharged then you will fall sick.

Energy Moving Meditation Series #8

MEDITATION GALORE

Our body is the most powerful machinery for the generation of power and increases its strength continuously, if worked upon in a scientific manner. But it is rarely that we feel the importance of the body for helping us out.

The following pages will provide you with lot of techniques for releasing the energy blocks from various parts of the body without much strain or hard work. These energy blocks develop due to

- Tension
- Stress
- Pollution
- Lack of sleep
- Brooding

These techniques can be done at office also. For doing these techniques it is not necessary that every individual should have full concentration.

Technique #1

EARTH POWER

Stand with feet shoulder width apart.

The hands should be on the sides but the palms should be closed in a fist.

Harden the muscles of the thighs and calf. Slowly swing your body towards the front, the spine should be kept erect, move to the extent that you can balance perfectly and hold for a slow count of five.

Come back to the original posture. Repeat the above technique. In this case swing your body to the back, till you can balance comfortably.

This technique will provide you the energy to understand the basic centering region of your body.

Technique #2

SPINE POWER

Stand with feet shoulder-width apart.

The hands should be on the sides totally relaxed. Raise the arms to the shoulder levels and hold them there, palms facing the sky.

Turn waist to move the arms, when you reach the extreme, clinch the fist and hold the breathe for a count of five release and return to the process of twisting.

Technique #3

OPEN YOUR HEARTS

Stand with feet shoulder-width apart.

The hands should be on the sides loosely. Tighten the shoulders in such a manner that the shoulder plates meet together, hold the position for a period of ten slow count.

Repeat the process for five times. This will release the tensions stored in the hands, shoulders and back region.

Release all the tension and relax your hands on the sides.

Breathe in deeply and bring the left palm near the genital region and place the right palm over it. Let the fist formation of the both the hands happen.

Inhale deeply and tense the shoulder muscles and expand the hands outwards in such a manner that the shoulder plates touch each other. Exhale and bring the hands back to the level of the genital region.

Repeat the process for five times.

Technique #4

WEIGHT ENERGISATION

Stand in a normal manner, Spine and face erect with the hands on the sides.

1. Shift all weight of your body to the heel of one foot and tense the muscles of the same foot. Slowly inhale and exhale for a count of ten. Bring back the foot to normal position and repeat the process with other foot.

   Relax your body and count slowly to ten.

2. Raise the left foot as high as possible, balancing the whole body on the right foot. Hold for a count of ten, bring back the left foot to normal position and repeat the process with the right foot.

Relax your body and count slowly to ten.

3. The technique is similar to step 2, the only difference is that in this technique the raising of the leg will be done as if swinging the left leg from the front to the back of the body.

   Relax your body and count slowly to ten.

4. Raise both the hands in front of you, tense the fingers of the hands, and convert them into fist. Tense all the muscles in the hand from palm to the shoulders. Count slowly from 1 to ten.

   Relax your body and count slowly to ten.

5. This step is similar to step 4 except that in this case the palms are raised and lowered as if flapping the hands. Repeat this process for ten times and relax the body. Count slowly to ten.

   Relax your body and count slowly to ten.

6. This step is similar to step 4 except that in this case the palms are turned into a fist and rotated in a circular motion, ten times slowly in a clockwise direction and ten times slowly in anti-clockwise direction.

   Relax your body and count slowly to ten.

Technique #5

LUNG POWER

This is a power bearing technique and should be done only by people who have strong lungs and breathing capabilities.

For doing this technique

Stand with feet shoulder-width apart.

Inhale deeply exhale deeply, keep the hands on the sides of the body.

After ten round slow breathing begin the process of Meditative breathing.

For doing this inhale deeply raise both the hands to the level of the chest join the palms together in such a manner that the fingers of both the hands touch respectively (in India it is called Namaskar postion)

STEP #1

With the inhalation chant mentally AUM (ॐ) and feel the flow of the mantra through your mouth to the throat and from the throat to the lungs.

During the process of the chant of AUM concentrate on the Navel centre and feel the fire in the belly rising up to receive the eternal primordial sound.

Release the breathe forcefully by saying AAAAA.............. through the mouth.

Close the mouth and Inhale deeply by chanting HUMMMMM....., Hold the breath and feel the intense sensation building up in the throat area.

STEP#2

Repeat step # 1 four times.

STEP#3

Repeat the step #1 but in this the concentration of the body should be at the Mooladhara/ Base Chakra level.

Mentally visualise a dark coloured wheel rotating in the Mooladhara chakra. Let the colour of the chakra change from dark colour to reddish orange and the speed of the rotation also increase considerably.

Similarly let the colours change from reddish-orange to yellow and the speed of the chakra increase by four times. Now relax and close your eyes, if feel trembling sensation, you can lie down.

Regular practice of this meditation will force the Kundalini to awaken.

❋❋❋

Thinking about Meditation with open Eyes will not create a Sadhaka, Practice with devotion and faith and You would realise your own destiny soon

Visual meditations

Visualisation is a powerful technique that requires basic skills as well as developed visual skills.

The meditations in section are written in such a manner that if practiced for longer period of time the meditator would be able to do Visual meditation without difficulty.

Visual meditation is a process of developing the concept of visualisation in such a manner that it is easier for the practitioner to gauge the depthness of the problem in an easier manner.

Benefits of Visual Meditation

- Better level of concentration.
- Better level of conceptualization and development.
- Better analysis of a problem
- Better recall value.
- Better and sustained level of mental growth.

Visual Meditation #1

POWER VISUALISATION

Sun - the star that has been revered and worshipped for million of years and is one of the most powerful sources of energy without which nobody can survive.

Sit comfortably in a room, with all the curtains drawn. This will create darkness in the room - first thing we want to have is the Sun to come into our room.

Concentrate on the wall in front of you and mentally draw a Sun with all the features of it on the wall. After drawing the sun colour it with the blazing light colour of the Yellowish-Red.

Let this sun of yours become brighter and brighter like the nature's own creation.

Note: In the beginning it is quite possible that the visualisation may not be so effective, but with practice and preseverance effort the results would be surprising.

BENEFITS

a. The power of concentration will increase with this meditation

b. The visualisation power will increase

c. Balancing of both sides of the brain will happen.

Visual Meditation #2

DUPLICATE

Every individual has two sides of psychology, one that is positive and the other negative. This meditation will help you to diffuse these two sides in one and also help you to take the decision regarding the side you want to take on.

For doing this technique you would require mirror or standstill water. Sit near the mirror or the water in such a manner that your reflection is clearly visible.

Look into the reflection delving deep into the eyes of the reflection. See the hatred, envy, jealousy, impatience in the eyes, look at the body language of the reflection. See the super ego complex in the reflection.

Look again into the reflection delving deep into the eyes of the reflection. See the love, care, understanding, patience in its eyes, look at the body language of the reflection. See the caring good-natured complex in the reflection.

Let the two reflections separate and you will be able to find the good and the bad self. Let the negative self move towards the left and the good nature move towards the right.

Now begin the comparison in true sense. Let the two reflections show their own faults and their strengths. The more you are able to get closer to the reflections the more you will understand yourself.

The moment the reflection on the left sides merges with the reflection on the right side, you will accept the positive aspects of life, while in the other case you will be accepting the negative aspects of life.

The more this meditation is done the more and better person we will become. Now let both the reflection merge to become one, and you will see a definite change in you after this meditation.

Visual Meditation #3

BATHING IN THE COSMIC LIGHT

Life is an energy that flows through us, it is because of this spark that we are able to move and are considered to be living. The moment this spark leaves us, the physical form of the body may remain but without life.

Yogic practitioners from the ancient times had accepted that this spark is the divine force that changes bodies like changing of clothes and resides in a particular body for a specific period of time to accomplish a specific task assigned to it by the divine energy.

The purpose of this meditation is two-fold:

- Help you to understand the flow of the energy residing in the body
- To be able to energise this divine force so that it works as per our requirements and to show us the exact path to be followed.

STEP#1

For doing this meditation sit in a comfortable place and take deep but slow breathes. Feel the flow of energy in the reverse direction of the spinal column. Let the energy flow from the base of the spine to the top of the spinal column..

Continue this process for ten times

STEP#2

Close your eyes and feel that the energy so reaching the top of the spinal column flowing out to the brain. Let it flood the brain fully so that it overflows.

The overflowing energy, which is Golden in colour, is covering the face, neck, chest, abdomen, genital area, thighs, calves, ankles and feet. The moment the energy reaches the feet let it flow back from the feet to the spinal column and process continues.

Sit in this process of divine bath of light till you feel comfortable.

Regular practice can help you to cleanse all the chakras with this divine energy.

Visual Meditation #4

SO-HAM
(I am He)

This is a powerful technique that helps you to get in touch with the divine energy and also provides a sample of vast and beautiful cosmos.

For doing this technique sit comfortably and close your eyes. Place both your hands over the navel, the right palm over the left palm. Do deep breathing for a few times.

Now visualise your entire body getting transformed into a egg shaped light. Let this cosmic egg expand till it covers the entire room. Continue to expand your body till it exceeds all the limits set down by human standards. Now it is the size of the whole of the cosmos itself, the divinity of yours is all encompassing. You may feel that the house you reside is nothing but a speck in the whole cosmic self of yours. The city, state, country and even the whole world is nothing more than a fraction of your whole self.

Stay in this divine self of yours till the time you feel comfortable. You can also create and change things in this divine cosmos. One important thing to understand is that a tiny fraction of change will affect you and every other organism within this divine self to change permanently.

With this all encompassing self of yours imagine the responsibility and accountability that lies with you. Every single movement of yours changes the cosmos in a particular manner.

You can continue to experiment with this energy and whenever you want to reduce this cosmic light of yours change to body's size.

Bow down in reverence, to the divine energy for

managing this cosmos without a single error or rectification for billions of years.

Regular practice of this meditation will provide the following benefits:

- The practitioner will get the ability to take on the responsibility of daily life without any difficulty.
- The dreadful feeling related with owning responsibility will subside.

Visual Meditation #5

DIVINE ENERGY SHOWER ME WITH YOUR LOVE

- For doing this sit down comfortably, close your eyes and place your hands in a worship posture.

With the closed eyes mentally visualise the Divine Energy in the form you have always worshipped. The detailed visualisation should be perfect with every detail, be it the clothes, expression of the face etc.

Once you have visualised the Divine energy in the form of worship by you, feel that a divine light is flowing out from the heart of the divinity.

Let this divine light flow to you hearts in the subtlest manner. It may be possible that you will feel warmth of the divine in the heart region. Sit in this position till the time you want.

This technique is simple and effective and it balances the Anahata Chakra in a few seconds.

❋❋❋

Anna dies leaving the poor Patrick, a wealthy widower. He feels relived and asks the Undertaker, the cost of burying his wife.

"Rs. 5000/-" replied the undertaker. Patrick requests for a discount and the undertaker say the minimum he can charges is Rs. 3500/-.

"My God!" wails Patrick, counting out his money, "I almost wish she was still alive!, she was much cheaper"

Even Death leaves sadness and agony around for long.

Contemplation meditation

Contemplation is a process of pondering over a thought with an anticipation of getting some valid results.

This contemplation be it in negative direction or positive direction yields results. The outcome of the

techniques will be totally dependent on the way a person works towards the goal.

In this section I have covered some important meditation techniques that requires more personal attention for the practitioner and also provides an option of working towards the goals in suitable manner.

- For all the following meditation, sit comfortably in a place, with closed eyes.
- Breathe in deeply hold and release. Continue this process for ten times. The breathing should be slow and restrained.

Contemplation Meditation #1

UNION OF NATURE & PURUSHA

- Concentrate on the gap between the inhalation and exhalation.

- The gap will provide a space to delve deeper into your own supra-conscious mind. The deeper you delve the awareness about the union of the Prakriti (Nature) and Purusha (Supreme being) will dawn upon you.

Contemplation Meditation #2

DIVINE ENERGY

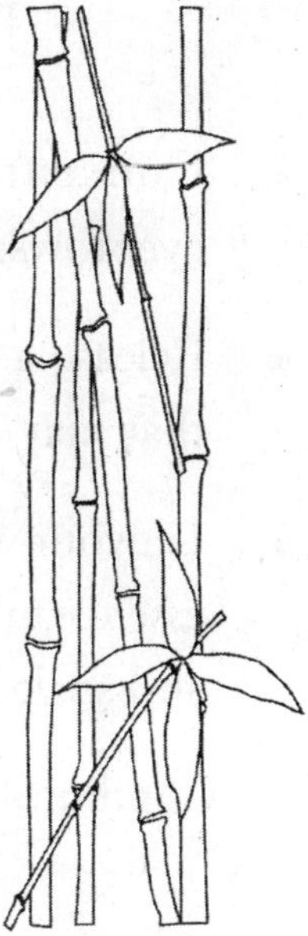

- With every deep exhalation concentrate on heart region, let all your thoughts and matter disappear with the divine love in the heart.
- After a certain time the breathing stops on its own (donot worry as by this time you would be in a state of deep meditation).
- At this juncture you are a pure soul with one you were born. This is the pure power of Shakti (Goddess).
- The movement of this energy will be subtle and fast. You will feel surrounded by sensations that you have never felt before.

- This energy stops at certain points before awakening fully; it is called the rise of Kundalini Shakti.

Contemplation Meditation #3

THIRD EYE POWER

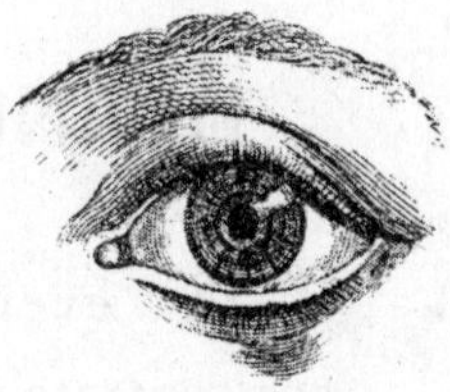

- Concentrate between your eyebrows.
- Release all the thought processes that may creep up.
- Let your whole body be filled with the cosmic breath essence up to the top of your head and remain there, and soak in radiant spatiality.

Contemplation Meditation #4

SENSES FOR YOU

- Visualise a peacock feather; see all the five colours of it.
- These five colours are your five major senses (Seeing, Hearing, Smelling, Tasting and Feeling).

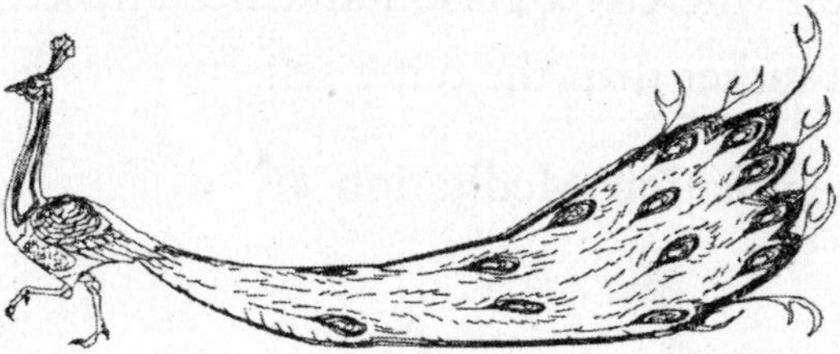

- Discard all the five senses by surrendering yourself to the unlimited love hidden in the spatiality of your own heart.

Contemplation Meditation #5

I AM THE ONE

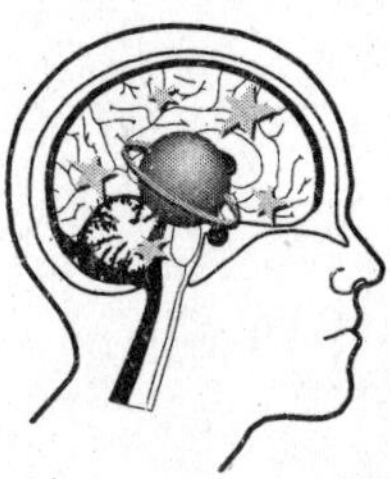

- Close your eyes and feel as if the whole cosmos is absorbed in your own head.
- Gaze inwards to sense the true divine nature of yours.

This meditation would provide a sense of fulfillness in the mind of the practitioner and also develop a keen sense of understanding of the nature.

The next meditation is an extended form of this

meditation whereby a person attaches himself with his inner self rather than the outer self.

Contemplation Meditation #6

ONE WITH THE COSMOS

- Let the index fingers of both the hands close the both the eyes, thumbs fingers close both the ears, middle finger close both the nostrils and ring finger close the mouth.

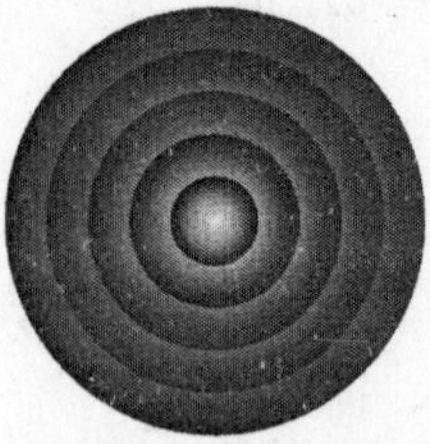

- Meditate on its internal vacuity, the infinite space between your eyebrows.

Contemplation Meditation #7

TU HI TU

- Tilt your head to face the sky, close both the ears with both the index fingers.
- Place the tongue on the upper palate

- Concentrate on the space between the eyebrows and you will hear the supreme sound of (ॐ) AUM resounding in your own consciousness.
- Merge with the sound till you are not there and the feeling of oneness with the nature doesnot occur.

Contemplation Meditation #8

AUM (ॐ)

- Visualise AUM (ॐ) in totality and concentrate on it. Let the tongue touch the upper palate and bring the awareness to the space between the eyebrows.
- Bring the AUM to the space between the eyebrows.

Contemplation Meditation #9

SOUND SENSATION

- Concentrate your mind on any sound and feel the slow rising and falling rhythm.

- Let the concentration bring the sound into your heart and then when the sound becomes one discard it and you will be in a state of ecstasy.

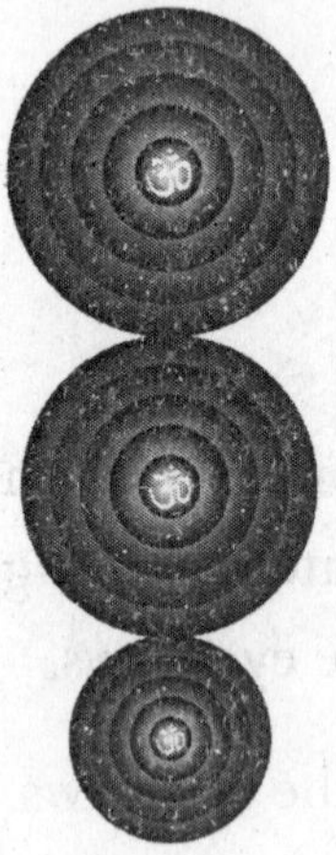

Contemplation Meditation #10

WORD SENSATION

Repeat the above meditation replacing the sound with visualisation of a word.

The word can be any religious symbol or mantra but caution should be taken that long mantra are not taken as it would be difficult to contemplate and visualize.

Once a person is able to realise the potential of sound and rhythm then every other ingredient of nature would automatically fall into the lap of the practitioner.

Contemplation Meditation #11

OH MY HEART

- Concentrate your mind in your heart while engaged in worldly activity.
- This will remove the agitation and in a few days the indescribable will happen.

Contemplation Meditation #12

FIRE SENSATION

- Let your whole self be covered with the fire that burns in your own body.
- Let this fire burn you down till nothing is left and ashes scattered by the wind, try to know the tranquility of space that returns to space.
- This is the moment of true awareness and also of reckoning.

Contemplation Meditation #13

SENSATION

- Bring the hands at the shoulder level, and let your breath flow through all the pores of the arms.
- Continuous breathing will generate a radiance that gradually pervades the armpits, ravishes the heart.
- It will bring the awareness in the Heart, Navel and the Base region.

Contemplation Meditation #14

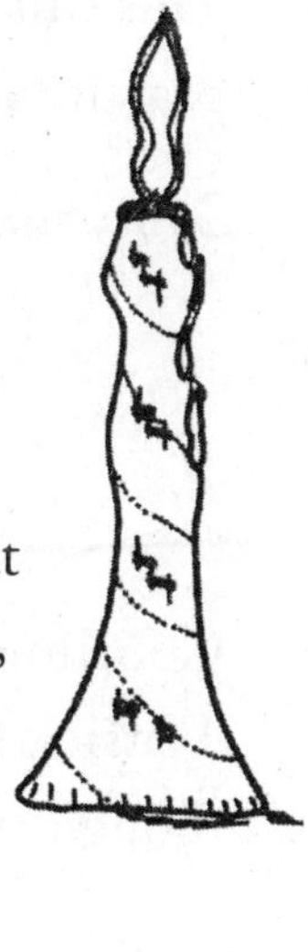

POWER GAZING

- Continuous and steady gazing without blinking at a pebble, a piece of wood, or any other ordinary object will bring awareness to inner self.

Contemplation Meditation #15

HA

- Slightly part your mouth and continue to breath deeply.
- Bring your awareness to the tip of the tongue and when you exhale, exhale with a sound of HA.
- This will balance all the emotional symptoms in the practitioner.

Contemplation Meditation #16

ENDLESS SKY

- Continuously gaze at the sky without blinking. Tensions Blood pressure and other upsetting thoughts will disappear.

- This technique can also be done before starting any other meditation.

Contemplation Meditation #17

WITHDRAWAL

- Look at an object intentionally for a few minutes.
- Then slowly close your eyes and then withdraw your thoughts and become the receptacle of ineffable plenitude.

Contemplation Meditation #18

HAMSA

- Deeply inhale and exhale for ten times.
- On the eleventh exhalation, exhale with the sound of SA. Inhale the breath with the sound HAM.
- Exhale with SA and continue with this technique for 108 times.

- If this technique is repeated for 195 days it is possible to get psychic powers endowed by the Goddess.
- This technique can be day and night. Only restriction is that non-vegetarian foods are not allowed.

❋❋❋

A woman decided to have her portrait painted. She told the artist, "Paint me with diamond rings, a diamond necklace, emerald bracelets, a ruby broach, and gold Rolex." "But you are not wearing any of those things," he replied. "I know," she said. "It's in case I should die before my husband. I'm sure he will remarry immediately, and I want his new wife to go crazy looking for the jewelry."

Anticipation of future has caused more tension than the future itself.

Advanced Techniques for Practioners

Balancing the Centre with the Nature Earth Meditation

It is an ancient meditation technique and mostly it is done before the healing or balancing was done. If a person is able to get perfection in this technique then he can have control over the Earth energy situated in the body for the beginning and latter is able to get the intuitive capability of knowing directions, flow of water, metallic objects under the earth.

On the physical level this technique helps in rejuvenation, physical regeneration, and long life.

Equipments required : A Compass, Rug

Time : Morning 4-7 Am
Evening 10-11 PM

- Locate the exact direction of north/south of the room.
- Lie down flat on your back with your body aligned north/south. The head should be towards the south. You should have a rug underneath you.
- Relax your body from top of the head to the tip of the toe. Slightly part your lips and let there be distance of one foot between the legs. The ankle can be placed at a comfortable angle and the neck also can be made comfortable by turning to a side.
- Slowly breath the count can be 1...2...3...4 for inhalation and the same for exhalation. Continue doing this for ten minutes.
- During the breathing allow the breathing to expand throughout your body. After five or six minutes you feel as if the whole body is breathing.
- Now mentally feel that your whole body is dissolving into the rug and there is no difference between you and the rug. Go on merging with it in such a manner that you feel the floor on which

the rug is placed. You can sense the coldness of the floor.

- Feel your body just becoming the part of the floor on which you are lying on. Go on merging with it feel the hard floor (in a room) melting into the soft earth below. Just let it go and let the soft earth envelope your whole body.
- Just go on merging with the whole of the earth in a way that you have become earth itself.
- The moment you achieve this state you will feel a leviathan experience and you will have the sensation that you are suspended somewhere in vacuum.
- You are aware of sounds and lights around you but unable to clearly relate to them. If you have really achieved this state then you can feel yourself spinning like the earth on its axis. The lower portion of the body will have more sensation compared to upper part of the body as it is facing the North direction. This will help you to balance the lower part of the body and also align it with the energy centers of the planet called Earth.
- If this method has reached a level of perfection you can actually feel that the whole body has changed its direction and the head will face the northern direction. Let the upper part of body also

get the similar kind of experience and this will energize the upper part of the body.

- **Note:**
    - o You can do this meditation for as long as you wish.
    - o The more the better but if there is any discomfort then start doing fast breathing 1 inhale and 1 exhale twenty times. Join the legs and tense the whole body and immediately open the eyes. Lie for a couple of minutes so that the body comes back to normal then you can getup.
    - o Do not drink water for at least half an hour after meditation.

Power of Spirit
The Contact with the Inner Self

Time: Between 06.00-12.00 hrs

ॐ Sit or lie down comfortably and inhale and exhale deeply for two-three minutes.

ॐ Close your eyes

ॐ Slow down your breathing to reach a state of oneness with inner self. How? Let the inhalation be done in the count of 4 the speed should

be like 1….2…..3…..4……, exhalation should also be done in the count of 4 i.e. 4……3…..2…..1….

ॐ This process should be done for a total round of ten.
  - This method will relax the mind and will help in reaching to the state of blankness.
  - This breathing pattern will also help in draining out the worries and tensions. The more the draining happens the more you shall be ready for the meditation in a proper manner

ॐ Feel the Earth below you and allow yourself to sink into it until you reach a state where you are cradled in a small shallow ground.
  - Let the whole body of yours relax further and surrender yourself to Mother Earth as in her lap no harm can come to you.
  - The more you relaxed you feel the Mother Earth covering you in her folds, protecting you, draining out all those things which can drain you or harm you in her own folds.

ॐ The moment you are relaxed you will feel new lease of energy flowing through the base of your spine in to the body, this is the energy of life and will nourish every single part of you. This experience is similar to plants which get energy and nourishment from the Mother Earth.

ॐ Go on inhaling and exhaling deeply and now you have to be attentive to the breath.

- Stage # 1
  - o You yourself shall feel that the breathing has slowed down to an extent of nearly stopping.
  - o The slowing of the breath can be felt by hearing subtle sounds that arises in the room, in the next room, in the house, just outside the window. A stage occurs that you are able to sense even the breathing of people walking, moving, sleeping in your room or even next room.
  - o This is exciting phase when you are able to synchronize the breathing of yours with one of the persons near you. Hear nothing except the breathing and continue to match the breathing pattern the more relaxed you become the more relaxed would be the breathing of the person nearby. All the tensions and worries would be automatically drawn into the earth,
- Stage # 2
  - o In this stage your awareness is to be limited to yourself draw your attention from the neighbour's breathing to your own breathings.
  - o The more attentive you become of the breathing

i.e. deep inhalation and deep exhalation the breathing slows down. It is true that the mind will be able to trace some voice, breathing patterns in the vicinity donot block them let the mind hear it and let it fade away, the more the voices fade away the more relaxed you become.

- This is a crucial position as at this juncture it is quite probable that Mother Earth will make you feel as if you are floating and the whole Mother Earth is enveloping like a quilt. You may feel like you are covered with wet soft earth and the warmth is insulating you to a great extent. Remain in this state as much as possible.
- The more you are relaxed the better warmth will be provided by the Mother Earth's Quilt.
- Hear yourself breathing, and feel the connection you have to the earth and to the seasons. And know that what affects them affects you, and that what affects you affects them.
- Let the breathing slowly come back to normal, and the awareness of other sounds begin to be felt again

Slowly open your eyes and become fully, awake, but still completely relaxed, and know that you have been cleansed and renewed for the year to come.

Antar Sabda The Voice of the Supra consciousness

Morning Meditation : Time : 05.00-0700 hrs

Before sitting for meditation say a brief prayer to God and Guru, invite them to be with you during your meditation.

Sit comfortably with the spine straight and eyes closed.

1. Place hands on the knees.

2. Practice deep slow relaxed breathing for a few minutes. Count the breath in 1...2...3...4 hold for a count of 1 then count the breath out 1...2...3...4. Do this for ten times.

3. Now let the breath flow in and out naturally (without counting). Mentally keep watch over the breath as it is coming in, just observe your thoughts, feelings between the gaps of inhalation and exhalation and also observe the thoughts and feeling during the exhalation.

Note: - Do not pre-determine or pre-conceive the thoughts as it would be dangerous.

In the beginning thoughts will flow in naturally let it come and go just watch them. Do nothing; do not get perturbed by anything.

If the thought is disturbing then just note and ignore it. Do this for ten minutes

4. Now inhale for a count of 1,2,3,4 and mentally say "OM" or "Ah-men" or "So-hum". Hold the breath for a count of 4 and release. Do this for ten times.

5. Now while inhaling say 'Aummmmmmm', or 'Ah-mennnnnnnnnnnn' or 'So-hmmmmmmmmmmmm'

This extension should be done till you feel a pressure building up in your chest area and then hold. Concentrate on the extension of 'mmmmmmm' or 'nnnnnnnnn' and you will feel a sensation happening. When the sensation stops release the breath from mouth slowly. Again close the mouth and repeat the process for ten times.

6. Now while inhaling say 'AAAAAAAAAAA' 'uuuuuuuuuuu' 'mmmmmmmmmmmmmmmm', or 'Ahhhhhhhhhhhhh'-'meeeeeeeee' 'nnnnnnnnnnnnnn' or 'Sooooooooo'-'huuuuuuuuuuu' 'mmmmmmmmmmmm'.

In this section each of the extension constitutes one cycle. For example while inhaling say 'AAAAAAAAAAA' this extension should be done till you feel a pressure building up in your chest area and then hold.

Concentrate on the extension of 'AAAAAAAAAAAA' and you will feel a sensation happening. When the sensation stops release the breath from mouth slowly. Again close the mouth and while inhaling 'uuuuuuuuuuuu' feel the pressure building up in the chest area and then hold. Concentrate on the extension 'uuuuuuuuuuuu' and you will feel the sensation happening.

When the sensation stops release the breath from mouth slowly. Again close the mouth and while inhaling 'mmmmmmmmmmmmmmm' feel the pressure building up in the chest area and then hold.

Concentrate on the extension 'mmmmmmmmmmm' and you feel the sensation happening. Repeat the process for ten times.

7. Inhale and exhale normally for a count of 1,2,3,4 for ten times.

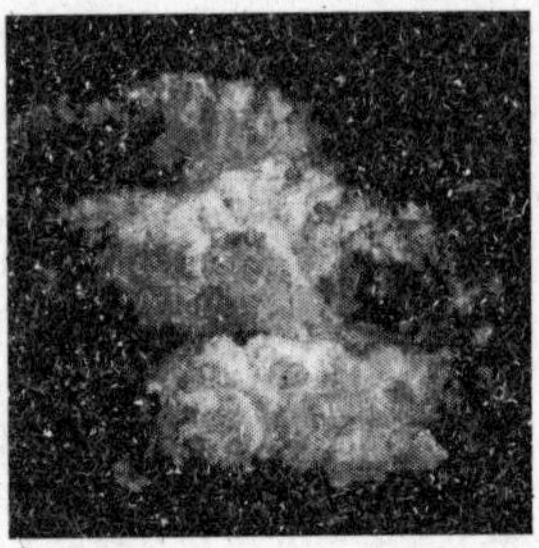

8. Say your prayers before opening your eyes.

Evening Meditation:

Time : 22.00-00.00 hrs

- Before sitting say a brief prayer

to God and Guru, invite them to be with you during your meditation.

- Sit comfortably keeping spine straight and eyes closed. Place the hands on the knees.
- Inhale and Exhale for a count of 4. Do this for ten times.
- Now breathe deep and fast through your nose continuously. Allow your body to move freely as you breathe. You can move your hands up and down or front and back while doing this meditation or any other physical motion that helps you pump more oxygen into your lungs.
- Start with one minute duration only and slowly expand for five minutes.
- **Note:** if somebody has breathing problem or cardiac problems please check with doctor before doing this exercise or you may do the breathing slowly and when you feel heat starting to develop. Stop and relax.

The following section should be done after the night meditation so that you may be able to sleep peacefully.

- Simply lie down on the bed.
- Spread the legs giving a comfortable gap and the

hands should be placed on the sides of the body in a comfortable position.

- Start breathing slowly. Focus your attention on your breath. Notice your breathing. Feel the breath as you inhale and as you exhale. In the beginning the breathing will be fast because of the meditation exercise done earlier and later the force slows down.
- In this exercise no control is there only have the feel of the breathing. The feeling should be of only for inhalation and exhalation. There is no right or wrong way to do this exercise.
- As you inhale, imagine you are inhaling peace and calmness. As you breathe out, imagine you are exhaling all the tensions of the day.
- Mentally concentrate on a part of body and ask it to get relaxed. For example, notice the muscles of your face and then ask these muscles to relax, repeat this for other parts of the body till you reach the feet.
- **Note:** When the concentration reaches the heart region say the following affirmation
    - ❖ I want the Heart region to open
    - ❖ Let the heart open to the beauty that is there in the world

- ❖ Let the Blessing of the Lord and Guru be with me for life
- ❖ Let the Heart open to the love for one and all.

Continue to focus your attention on your breathing until you fall asleep.

Power Channeling

The best timing for the meditation is :-

Time :

Morning : 0500-0700 IST

Night : 2200-2300 IST

Step 1

- Lie down on your back and relax.
- When you lie down have a rug or a blanket underneath.
- The legs should be one foot apart.
- The base of the feet should be relaxed.
- The hands should be on the sides and relaxed.

Step 2

- Inhale for a count of 1 and exhale for a count of 1

Step 3

- Inhale for a count of 4 and exhale for a count of 4

Step 4

- Inhale for a count of 4 and exhale for a count of 1(When you exhale, push the energy or the prana from your lungs to the lower abdomen 2 inches below navel.)

Step 5

- Inhale for a count of 4 and exhale for a count of 2 (When you exhale, push the energy or the prana from your lungs to the lower abdomen 2 inches below navel.)

Step 6

- Inhale for a count of 4 and exhale for a count of 4 (When you exhale, push the energy or the prana from your lungs to the lower abdomen 2 inches below navel.)

Note:-

A In the beginning the stomach may bulge out while inhaling. This should be avoided.

B Do not tense the muscles of the stomach as this would lock the energy in the stomach region

C For a better result in the beginning you can

hold in the abdominal muscles till the time you could coordinate the muscle with the breath.

D While inhaling caution should be taken for the speed as it should be slow otherwise there will be tension in the stomach region.

E Another helping method in the beginning is to keep the hands over the abdomen and press lightly while breathing in.

F Till you enjoy the meditation, continue and when the body shows that it is tired due to fulfillment of up the required energy. Stop at that and do not push yourself further as it shall damage other subtle nerves in the hip and groin region.

Centering Meditation

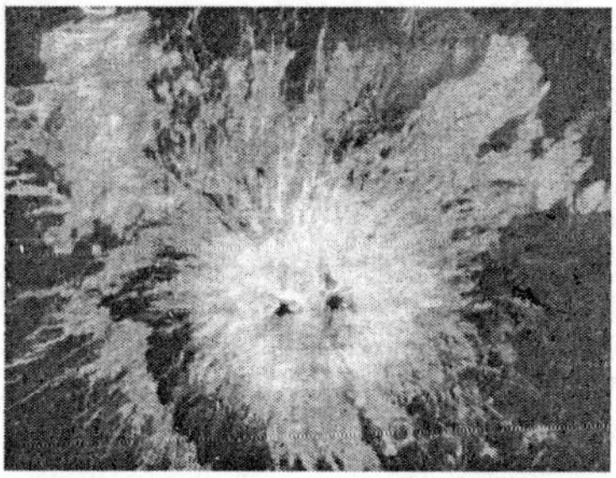

Time :

Best : 0400- 0600 hrs

Medium : 0600- 1000 hrs

Low : 1000- 1100 hrs

Step 1

Sit comfortably and keep the spine straight, during the whole process

- Close your eyes.
- Inhale for a count of 2 hold for a count of 2 and exhale for a count of 2.
- Do this for ten times

Step 2

- Inhale for a count of 4 hold for a count of 4 and exhale for a count of 4.
- Do this for ten times

Step 3

- Inhale for a count of 8 hold for a count of 8 and exhale for a count of 8.
- Breathe slowly and naturally.
- Do this for ten times.

Note :-

Please do this meditation after having medical advice from a medical expert if breathing problem or any other medical problem is there.

Important : While Inhaling or Exhaling, keep the mouth closed and only nose should be used for the breathing.

- You will feel a sense of peace flowing through your whole body; a relaxed nature would be achieved.

- If you do not feel relaxed then repeat the whole process again. If you are able to achieve it in the first round do not be worried as the more you are relaxed the better you shall be.

For help you can use sound to center yourself. Just sit quietly and ring a small bell or chimes.

Focus on the sound and breathe deeply. Keep making the sound until you feel centered.

Easy Power

Time : 5 am - 7:30 am
Duration : 10 - 15 minutes in total.

There are two parts A & B in this meditation. Part A will balance and centre the person, Part B will release stress.

Part A

1. Start by making sure you're sitting upright. Take three long, deep, slow breaths. Breathe in 4 seconds, breathe out 4 seconds. Do this for 10 counts. When you have finished, just allow your breathing

to return to normal.

2. Without trying to control the breath at all, just allow yourself to breathe normally through the nose.
3. Now gently become aware of the breathing. Gently watch the breath as it comes and goes. Follow the breath in and breath out.
4. Close your eyes and continue this for 60 seconds or so now. When you've finished, end the meditation by taking a deep breath.

Part B

1. As you're sitting there now, just gently squeeze your hands into fists....Take a few moments to really feel the tension.
2. Then, after a few seconds, let of all the tension in your hand completely.
3. Pause for a moment and notice the difference between the state of tension and the state of relaxation.
4. Now do the same with your toes and hands together. Gently curl your toes and clench your hands into fists. Hold on to that tension for a few seconds. And let go, releasing that tension completely.
5. Repeat again, this time tense your thighs and calf

muscles of the leg along with your toes and hands. Feel that tension for a moment. And again, let go of all those muscles, letting them relax completely.

Ground Activity Developing Chi

Time : 4 am - 6 am

Frequency of Practice : Thrice a week

Steps #1

1. Sit or Stand and be comfortable.
2. You may keep your eyes open or closed.
3. Get into a rhythmic breathing pattern - Inhale slowly and deeply for 4 seconds, do not stop, and exhale slowly and deeply from your stomach for a count of 4 seconds. Do this 10 times.
4. Establish the rhythm and feel relaxed.

Visualization :

1. Imagine **Roots** leaving from your body through your feet going deep down into the earth, **slowly penetrating into the core of the earth**. Breathe normally.

2. When you inhale, imagine the **Green Positive Energy** coming into your body from the established roots of the Core of the Earth, up from your feet, through your legs into the Dan Tien. The Dan Tien is the area 1.5 inches to 2 inches below the navel –between the Swadhisthana and the Mooladhara Chakras.
3. Allow the **Green Energy** to envelop you and let it be in every cell of your body from the toes to the head, the hair, in your skin. Bathe in this **Green Energy.**
4. Exhale, imagining **Red Energy** going out of your Mouth. This **Red Energy** is all the accumulated **Negative energy** in this life and in the past birth cycles.

Feel the exhaustion, tiredness, anger, sadness, desolation, sickness, desperations, frustrations being blasted from your system through your mouth into the space.

5. Allow more and more **Green Energy** to be pumped into your system, feel the soul getting refreshed and rejuvenated. Feel happy, elated in joy and feel **Centered to the Earth.** Feel the calmness, the power developing inside you, feel the energy moving from your legs, up your thighs, through

the spine, into your heart, Lungs, stomach, arms, neck. Feel the energy surging into your head, into your eyes, ears and allow <u>**The Green Aura**</u> to surround you and be in this state of rejuvenation.

6. When you feel that there is no more **Red energy** coming out from your system and you have more than enough <u>Green Energy</u>, pull your anus up, breathe in, breath out and step aside from the original standing position or move your haunches from the original seating position.

Session Close

By this process you will go about accumulating the **Chi/ Energy** by which the body and soul gets recharged and rejuvenated. By listening deeply inside yourself you will feel and hear the **Chi** movements in your body. <u>**Listen and be aware of it.**</u>

When you have lots of **Chi**, you will never feel disassociated from the **Self.** You will be able to connect faster, be in peace and will be able to think and act clearly without any Duality. You will know what you have to do. This activity is a must for all of us to be in sync with the Energy enabling all of us to get activated for the tasks ahead.

Silencing the Mind #1

Concentrate on each line mentioned here and then do Concentration on it everyday for one week. The day for beginning the meditation is Sunday.

Controlling the Senses

This is essential for getting success in any meditation process

- Sit in a comfortable position
- Spine Erect
- Body relaxed- This can be easily done by slow and deep inhalation and exhalation for a count of 4.

First Day- Sunday

- Watch the fingers
- Watch the hand
- Watch the Wrist
- Watch the Elbow
- Watch the Area between Elbow and Shoulder
- Move the Fingers
- Watch the effect on the other parts of the hand
- Move the wrist
- Watch the effect on the other parts of the hand

- Move the hand
- Watch the effect on the other parts of the hand

Second Day- Monday

- Watch the Toe
- Watch the Ankle
- Watch the Knee
- Watch the Thigh
- Watch the Hip
- Move the Toe
- Watch the effect on the other parts of the Feet
- Move the Ankle
- Watch the effect on the other parts of the Feet
- Move the Knee
- Watch the effect on the other parts of the Feet
- Move the Thigh
- Watch the effect on the other parts of the Feet
- Move the Hip
- Watch the effect on the other parts of the Feet

Third Day- Tuesday

- Today you would do what you did on the First day and Second day but simultaneously concentrate on the hands and feet.
- Try to synchronize the movements between the feet and hand.

Fourth Day- Wednesday

- Repeat Third Day. While synchronizing the movement let the eyes move with the movement of the hand and feet.
- Try to hear any sounds that the body makes when movement take place

Fifth Day- Thursday

- Repeat Fourth Day.
- Now when you make movement tense your muscle and inhale. Let the muscle be tense and the breathing once inhaled should be held
- Now when you release the tension release the breathing
- Repeat this process for ten times.

Sixth Day- Friday

- Close your eyes and let the mind make your body movement work for you.
- Command the movement to happen and feel it happen

Seventh Day- Saturday

- Tighten all the muscles and inhale deeply and hold.
- While releasing let the breathe also be exhaled.
- Continue for ten times

The technique is simple yet very powerful and it can be done at any period of time even while sitting on a office chair. Be very attentive and see the results in one week.

Silencing the Mind #2
Controlling the Desires

This is the second part of the Silencing the Mind #1 and it should be only done after doing the first technique; otherwise you will not get positive results.

Concentrate on each line mentioned here and then do Concentration on it everyday for one week.

Note : People with medical problems should check with a medical practitioner before doing this technique

Process of doing this technique

Preliminary

- Place a rug (preferably made of wool or Silk if cotton is only choice then place the same above a blanket)

- Stand on the rug
- Spine Erect
- The hands on the sides
- Inhale slow and deep for a count of 4 and exhale for a count of 4 (three rounds)
- Relax and do normal breathing (three rounds)
- Inhale slow and deep for a count of 6 and exhale for a count of 6 (five rounds)
- Relax and do normal breathing (five rounds)
- Inhale slow and deep for a count of 10 and exhale for a count of 10 (five rounds)
- Relax and do normal breathing (five rounds)

First Step (Two minutes)

- Inhale deeply and hold
- Tighten the face muscles
- Tighten the shoulder muscles
- Tighten the hand muscles
- Tighten the chest muscles
- Tighten the stomach muscles
- Tighten the Thigh muscles
- Tighten the calf muscles
- Hold for a count of 5 and release
- Exhale slowly

Second (Two minutes)

- Inhale deeply
- Raise your hands towards the sky (stretch as far as possible)
- Raise the feet to touch the sky (the pressure is felt at the ankle, calf and
- thigh muscles)
- Hold for a count of 10 release
- Exhale slowly

Third Stage (Two minutes)

- Spread the legs (the distance between feet should be roughly 12 inches)
- Inhale for a count of 4 Hold and the moment you hold pull the anus up (in the beginning you can put strain on the stomach region to pull the anus in)
- Look towards the Sky with strain on the neck region (people who have neck problems should not do this step) for a count of 10
- Let the face come down in normal position
- Release the pressure on the anus
- Release the breath slowly

Fourth Stage (2 minutes)

- Keeping the same posture as in Third
- Place the right hand over the navel region

- Place the left hand behind the back (face of the palm touching the spine)
- Inhale normally for three rounds
- Pull the Anus in
- Inhale deeply for a count for 4
- And Say loudly 'HO' (the strain has to be felt at the navel region)
- Repeat the process

Fifth Stage

You can sit down and close your eyes and meditate or breathe normally till you feel comfortable.

Be very attentive and see the results in one week.

Preferred timing is morning before 8 and in night after 10. Please be sure that there is atleast a gap of 3 hours between meal and exercise otherwise it can damage the digestive system.

Silencing the Mind
Know Thyself

1. Sit comfortably on a chair or a cushion
2. If you are sitting on chair place the feet firmly on ground (place a rug under it) and if you are sitting on a cushion or floor be in Padmasana (put your

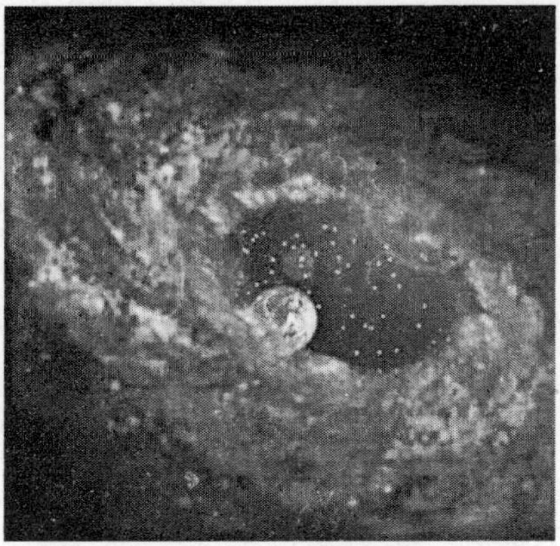

feet on opposite thighs. You may also sit simply with your legs tucked in close to your body), Siddhasana (place your right leg on your left thigh) Make sure that all the weight is distributed in a manner that supports you for some time.

3. The spine should be straight, keep it as straight as possible, the shoulders should also be firm. The balance should be made centering the abdomen. Slightly push your back towards the front, the head should be straight the chin should be at 90 degree in comparison to neck.
4. Slowly sway the upper body forward and backwards slightly with firmness. Slowly move the body from left to right, let this adjustment happen till you are in a comfortable position to sit and do the exercise.
5. Bring your gaze to the tip of the nose. Slowly raise the gaze towards the floor. Keep raising the

gaze till you feel the eyes are at a comfortable level.

6. Let the tip of the tongue touch the roof of the mouth and the lips should be closed.
7. The hands should be placed on the lap. The right palm should rest on top of the left palm and the thumb of left palm should touch the thumb of the right hand. The shape of the hands would be like a oval. The position of the palm should be near the navel region
8. Inhale and exhale for ten times. The breathing should be done as slowly as possible. You should be able to feel the breathing going to the lower abdomen do not force it, if done naturally then it would flow towards the lower abdomen directly
9. The attention should be on your breath if the mind wanders bring it back to breath. There should not be any movement in the body. The stillness should be there.
10. Slightly tighten the muscles of the leg and let the awareness flow into the abdomen and leg. The thoughts should be slowed by concentration on the breath.

Keep in this position for ten minutes or as much as possible.

11. Slowly relax the hands (bring them back to normal position), Relax the legs by stretching and on standing stretch the body as much as possible.

Last moment tips

These Tips are not exactly tips but are something that comes by regular practice and dedicated service to the universal energy.

Have you seen anybody dancing? He is totally aware of himself and dances his way in a manner as decided by his heart. Meditation is also similar to the dancer. You need not reach anyplace, you have to just delve deep in yourself to find the true self and be a Soul Searcher.

The dancer notices every emotion of the public but he does not get attached to the feeling, the moment he attaches importance to the emotion of the public, he will lose all his dedication to the dance. Similarly a meditator should be aware of all the flow of energy in and around him but will never get attached to it.

In the beginning many things may dissuade you from the practice of meditation, but it is important to understand and work through them.

I am providing some tips that if kept in mind which can help you to a great extent.

- In the beginning it is quite possible that the mind will not stay in one place that you require, it may wander here and there. Donot be dissuaded start the process again after taking few deep breathes.
- Never force yourself your mind to meditate. It is like a wild horse difficult to control in the beginning. The mind will try all the tricks to attract your attention. Let the thoughts and the illusions come and it is possible that for no reason you will feel itching and sneezing. Ignore it let it come and go but continue with the practice.
- In the breathing pattern remember to exhale more than the oxygen inhaled.

- **Remember** to find time for yourself. Even if you are able to spare ten minutes a day you will add up to whooping 3650 minutes or approximately 152 hours in a year.
- Remember Lord Krishna had said in the Grand Epic The Bhagawat Gita "Do your duties with full dedication and leave the results to me, I shall lead you towards the light", Similarly donot get disheartened if you are not finding results within a specified period of time.
- The results of the meditations with each practice session and period of dhyana will vary.
- **Remember** the universal energy is there to help you and guide you; you have to take the first step so that you can cross the ocean of knowledge to reach the true essence of being.

Please do write about your experiences after doing the meditational processes given in this book at the following address.

Soul Searchers
427, Dhruva Apartments,
Plot No. 4 I.P. Extension
Delhi-110092
http://www.soulsearcher.org

Other Books by R. Venugopalan

SOUL SEARCHERS - THE HIDDEN MYSTERIES OF KUNDALINI

Although the science of Kundalini existed for thousands of years, it is only in the recent years people have found fascination for this science.

In ancient period this science was only taught to those who had the ability to work upon this and was capable of spreading the knowledge to others. But today the need for this science is comparatively higher than in the ancient period.

This book will take you a step further into the secrets of all chakras present in the body - the major as well as minor nadis attached with them. This book will help you to solve many of the questions that have been lingering on the mind:

- What is the importance of each chakra?
- How are the chakras formed?
- Is chakra formation happening after birth or is decided before birth itself?
- If the decision of the chakras are made before the birth then what is the pattern of formation of the chakras?
- What is the significance of the Petals/ Nadis of a Chakra?
- Does tingling sensation mean the Kundalini has awakened?
- Is opening of chakra and Awakening of Kundalini same?
- What is the role of the nadis, Granthis and other energy centre in the body?
- Can one open chakras without activating Kundalini?
- Are there differences between various chakras? What is the importance of Minor chakras and Major-Minor chakras?

- Can Kundalini be awakened from a wrong direction?
- What are the different ways of awakening Kundalini Shakti?
- Can Kundalini be awakened from distance?
- Is it possible to give self-initiation? How?
- How does soul leave the body? What all it has to suffer before getting a new body ?
- What are sins, Karmas, and how they form a basis for the chakra development?
- Answers to many of the questions can be found in one book.

First time discloses

- **10 Major chakras, 300 Major-Minor Chakras, 237 Minor chakras, 180 Nadis, 16 Granthis and discloses the importance of each of the above categories in detail.**
- **Development of Chakra in the womb.**
- **Karma transfer, Sins and their punishments are covered in detail.**
- **Human Body** –Tridosha, Dhatus, Vayu, Tatva, Nadi Vigyan
- **Covering various nadis situated at *Face, chest, shoulder, stomach, Palms and base of Feet***
- **Balancing of Brahma, Vishnu and Rudra Granthi**
- **Kundalini Awakening Process-**
  - Shaktipata, Mantra Shaktipata, Mantra Sadhana, Swa-Diksha (Self Initiation), Through your own Body Strength
- **Active meditations and exercises for chakras**

• Roving Ball of Light, Die- Die to be Born Again, HAHA-HOHO-HEHE, Tatva Meditation, Visual Healing, Healers Mantra Technique, Navel Massage, Raj Kechari Mudra, Chakra Energisation Technique, Chakra Breathing

- **Yoga Postures Beneficial for Awakening of Kundalini**
  - *Bhujangasana, Shunya Dhara, Sharira Gyana, Surya Namaskar*

Pages: 443 Size 8 ½ " x 5 ¼ " Illustrations: 8 Colour Pages showing the Chakras and hundreds of black and white illustrations. Price: Rs. 175/-

SOUL SEARCHERS - THE ART OF BREATHING

Pranayama, Reiki, Visualisation, Crystal, Aura, Marma Gyana, Mudra, Asanas, Kundalini

'The Art of Breathing' is the beginning, the beginning of the new dawn in search of the true being 'The Soul'. This book is first of the series of a comprehensive and enlightening journey through the art of visualisation and breathing techniques. This book is amalgamation of the eastern science with the science of the west.

First time so many visual meditational techniques have been covered ranging from basic meditational techniques to advanced techniques.

Each section of the book gives explanation about the techniques beforehand so that the practitioners are able to get full information before beginning to use the techniques.

Visualisation Techniques

Beginners Level : Alpha Level, Formless Wanderer, Freedom from the Shackles, Inner Cleansing, More Visual Happiness, Self Introspection, Self Knowledge

Advanced Level : Sense of the Death, Sense of the Fire, Soul Torturer, Spiritual Awakening, Colour Meditation, Sense of the Void, Dance of Ecstasy, Past Life Fantasy

Kundalini Yoga (Theory)

Definition of the Chakras and the Nadis related with them Ida, Pingala, and Susumna Nadi and Disclosing 12 other main nadis. 7 Major Chakras and **Disclosing the 109 main minor chakras never done before**

Kundalini Yoga : Practical

Through the process of Visualisation:- Awakening each of the Seven Major Chakras that is from Mooladhara to Ajna Chakra. Complete Awakening of Kundalini

Reiki

Reiki I Techniques : Reiki basics, Reiki Ideals, Nature and Properties of Reiki, Process of Healing in Reiki. Attitude of Gratitude, Stages in

Reiki, Attunements, and there importance: Reiki I, Reiki II, Reiki III A and Mastership with symbols and there respective meanings. ***Meditational and healing techniques have been provided in each level of Reiki***

Reiki I Process for doing Self-treatment for Reiki I, One to one healing, Many on one healing, **Reiki II Techniques:** Sandwich energy, Mirror energy, Hands on healing with symbols, Distant Healing through Transformation, Photograph, Dummy, Timed Healing, Programming the Energy, Healing the Dead, Reiki Box, Group Healing, **Reiki Mastership Techniques:** Past Life Healing, Reiki in Partnership, Reiki Aura and Chakra Balancing

Disclosing the Technique of Tibetan Attunement for Reiki I, II, III A, B

Meditation for Development of Energy (Chi) Spot Energy Technique, Hum Technique, Load and Carry Technique

Yogic Kriyas & Mudra Vigyan

Tratak- The Way of a Yogi, **Asanas**:- Sukhasana, Vajrasana, Siddhasana, Padmasana, Cross Bow Asana, Sarva Sukha Asana, Shavasana

Pranayama:-Inner invocation, Calling to the Universal Soul, Art of breathing, Art of breathing for advanced students, Inner voice, Energy Burst,

Aura :-Definition of various Colours seen in Aura and there meanings. Development of the Auric bodies from childhood to adulthood. ***Various methods of seeing Aura:*** Flow with me, Check Me Out, Advanced Check Me Out

Marma Gyana

Crystals :-The method used by Atlantians for treating and healing people. **Exercises**: Crystal Ball Meditation, Crystal Meditation, and Crystal Grid Formation

Pages: 366 Size: 8 ½" x 5 ¼" Illustration: Colour and Black & White, Price: Rs. 175/-

SOUL SEARCHERS - THE HEALING POWERS OF PYRAMID

There are many books available in the market that talk about the concept of Pyramids and its related history but they restrict themselves to the standard history and rarely touch the mystical powers of the pyramid. The current book will take you into a realm of Techniques of Pyramids that has been rarely discussed or even delved. This is the first part of two-volume set, but the coverage has been done in such a way that each volume would be complete on its own terms.

The chapters in the book have been arranged in such a manner that a person begins from the basics of understanding what Pyramids are and then progresses to higher energy tapping levels of the Pyramids. The book is divided in two parts, first part covers the theoretical aspects of pyramids and the second delves deep in to the realm of activating the energies tapped in the pyramid.

Topics Covered in the Book

An Introduction to Pyramids-Brief How, What, Why of Pyramids???, Sources of Egyptian History, First Steps, Ancient Egyptian Gods, Wonderful Ancient Egyptians, Mummification and After Life Journey.

How the Pyramids Works & its Importance

The Power of Yantra, Tantra and Mantra

Indian Cosmic Pyramid- Sri Yantra, Construction of Sri Yantra

Photographs from the Land of Pharaoh

Techniques:

Pyramids Energy in Daily Use- Blank energy, Office Rest and Rejuvenation Technique, Pyramid Caps, Pyramids-Pyramid Formation, White Light Meditation, Violet Beam Technique, Wish Boxes- Galore

Mystical Pyramid Techniques - Natural Pyramid, Shat Kone Siddhi, Power of the Eastern Direction, Power Technique of Earth, Harness the Power of Pyramid (Cut & Use Pyramids)

Power Grids (16 power Girds have been covered)

Pages : 170 Size: 8 ½" x 5 ¼" Illustration: Colour and Black & White
Price : 80/-

ॐ is the Pranava sabda; the sacred syllable representing Brahma that is omnipotent, omnipresent, and omniscient. The Divine Brahma is incomparable so we have a symbol which is perfect and it represents both the nirguna (unmanifested) and saguna (manifested) aspect of the Divine.

Although ॐ is considered as a part of Hindu religion it crosses the realm of religion, caste and creed as it is the power of Sabda, the power which all of us can relate to in this physical body. It is made up of three Sanskrit letters A, U, M representing creation, preservation and destruction; this is the reason why it is also known as the Pranava Sabda or primordial sound. This divine combination of letters makes it a composite prayer in itself. If the recitation is properly done with proper pronunciation it can resonate throughout the body and ultimately enter one's own self 'The Soul'.

This small book covers diverse aspects of AUM in relation to various states of mind, koshas and provides various paths to realize the Pranava. And for easier elevation of mind to attune to the divine sabda.

An audio CD is provided which will help you in proper way of chanting as well as meditation.

Three Meditation charts are also provided which would help you to delve deeper in the divine Mantrā to gain beautiful insights.

A Divine symbol of AUM has been provided that can be placed at the worship place or at work place for reminding you continuously that the divinity is there for you at every moment of life.

If the methods provided in the book are followed with due faith and respect you would be able to reach the state of trance where the supreme consciousness can be attained. This is a moment of realization with the divine self where the worldly petty things give way to the knowing of the divineness of AUM.

ISBN: 81-8056-578-5
Book Code: BV-5824

Rudraksha is the divine gift of Lord Shiva for the benefit of humanity. Rudraksha means Tears of Rudra (Lord Shiva); they are the holiest items with mystical powers. For thousands of years people have been utilizing the beads for obtaining spiritual, material and medicinal benefits.

It is believed that one who wears Rudraksha is untouched by sins, and is protected from all impious deeds or thoughts. The natural Electromagnetic Properties of the Holy Rudraksha Beads have been found to improve concentration, focus and mental stamina.

As per Ayurvedic scriptures, wearing Rudraksha can have a positive effect on the heart, nerves, and is good for relieving a person from stress, depression, anxiety, palpitations, high blood pressure. For the spiritual seekers this is a blessing in disguise as the wearer of Rudraksha is able to achieve his goals faster; also the effects of the rituals become ten times more effective.

Rudraksha Benefits:

- Benefits of wealth, removes misfortune, gives purity, peace and stability of mind.
- Achievement of greater heights in material life, be it wealth, prosperity, success, power, creativity, intuition, family harmony; fearless life.
- It improves in general, one doesn't have to worry about zodiacal aspect of nine planets anymore.
- Rudraksha has the capability to change (karmic) behavior patterns, and make a person different and better person by which one stops making mistakes and misjudgments.

This kit has been designed in such a manner that the seeker is able to get dual benefit from it. One, he gains the knowledge of Rudraksha and secondly, he is able to implement the knowledge so gained. This kit contains within its fold:

- A book for gaining insights into various aspects of Rudraksha and also its various varieties with beautiful pictures. This includes the various remedies for the Nava grahas (Nine planets).
- A Rudraksha Mala for wearing.
- Ingredients required for cleansing of the Rudraksha Mala and a self cleansing process.

ISBN: 81-8056-579-3
Book Code: BV-5823

No one can make the choice except the self. Once we commit to travel on this path then it is only matter of time. For the destination is not the final halt but the ongoing experience of joy each day passing provides is truly blissful. This is the path of the divine bliss; just flow on this path and be merged into the divinity sought by many, for you to realize that the divinity is truly You.

For helping you unwind in a faster manner this kit comprises of:

- A enchanting audio meditational CD that shall enhance the ability of delving deeper with description for it.
- A Zen Garden with its own unique tools for you to understand the beauty in the emptiness.
- A Zen Garden 'How to Manual' showing various designs that can be created for better harmony, peace and prosperity.

ISBN: 81-8056-587-4
Book Code: BV-5831

This is the definition of Meditation in its true sense. Nothing is and can be matched with the divineness of the moment which meditation provides. All the evolution in life passes through three stages of grooming to reach the state of Samadhi:

'Silence' arising from the Meditation; this is the first stage. It moves at a fast pace bringing in a state of peace, happiness and bliss. This is the beginning of the inner silence.

'Know me state' this is the first hand knowledge of the rising moments of ecstasy in and around the body. This is the gradual awakening of life force in the body. This is actual beginning of the seeker where he attains the knowledge of the divinity in all things and also desires to grow deeper into the deeper realm of it. This is a state of endless flow of ecstasy as the moment becomes more and more precious.

'Blissful am I' state is the third state of achievement where the body and mind delve deep into the knowledge of the Soul thereby paving way for the merging of Atman (Soul) with the Parabrahma (Omnipresent, Omnipotent, Omniscient divine). This is a state of pure bliss and a state leading to realization.

This book is an active process of taking one from the state of material understanding to the state of supreme understanding using the mediums known and understood by the modern people. Simple pleasures of life are taken as medium to provide the way to the divinity of the life itself. What this book provides is a three way process:

- This book helps you to un-wind all that is loaded into your psyche and brings you closer to the divine energy hidden in your inner consciousness.
- Drop all the events. Drop everything you know. Drop all to find the truth. As the title says 'Drop It!' the purpose of this book is to allow you to know the ways of dropping all the dirt you have loaded over the years.
- How long does the journey take? It depends mainly on You.

You may not be able to change the past but the present if well lived shall shape the future.

ISBN: 81-8056-580-7
Book Code: BV-5822